A SEPARATION

Center Point
Large Print

**This Large Print Book carries the
Seal of Approval of N.A.V.H.**

A SEPARATION

KATIE KITAMURA

CENTER POINT LARGE PRINT
THORNDIKE, MAINE

This Center Point Large Print edition
is published in the year 2017 by arrangement with
Riverhead Books, an imprint of Penguin Publishing Group,
a division of Penguin Random House LLC.

The text of this Large Print edition is unabridged.
In other aspects, this book may vary
from the original edition.
Printed in the United States of America
on permanent paper.
Set in 16-point Times New Roman type.

ISBN: 978-1-68324-400-4

Library of Congress Cataloging-in-Publication Data

Names: Kitamura, Katie., author.
Title: A separation / Katie Kitamura.
Description: Center Point Large Print edition. | Thorndike, Maine :
    Center Point Large Print, 2017.
Identifiers: LCCN 2017008785 | ISBN 9781683244004
    (hardcover : alk. paper)
Subjects: LCSH: Married women—Fiction. | Marital conflict—Fiction. |
Adultery—Fiction. | Psychological fiction. | Large type books. | BISAC:
FICTION / Literary. | FICTION / Psychological. | FICTION / Family
Life.
Classification: LCC PS3611.I877 S47 2017b | DDC 813/.6—dc23
LC record available at https://lccn.loc.gov/2017008785

For Hari

A SEPARATION

1.

It began with a telephone call from Isabella. She wanted to know where Christopher was, and I was put in the awkward position of having to tell her that I didn't know. To her this must have sounded incredible. I didn't tell her that Christopher and I had separated six months earlier, and that I hadn't spoken to her son in nearly a month.

She found my inability to inform her of Christopher's whereabouts incomprehensible, and her response was withering but not entirely surprised, which somehow made matters worse. I felt both humiliated and uncomfortable, two sensations that have always characterized my relationship with Isabella and Mark. This despite Christopher often telling me I had precisely the same effect on them, that I should try not to be so reserved, it was too easily interpreted as a form of arrogance.

Didn't I know, he asked, that some people found me a snob? I didn't. Our marriage was formed by the things Christopher knew and the things I did not. This was not simply a question of intellect, although in that respect Christopher again had the advantage, he was without doubt a clever man. It was a question of things withheld, information that he had, and that I did not. In short, it was a question of infidelities—betrayal always puts one partner in the position of knowing, and leaves the other in the dark.

Although betrayal was not even, not necessarily, the primary reason for the failure of our marriage. It happened slowly, even once we had agreed to separate, there were practicalities, it was no small thing, dismantling the edifice of a marriage. The prospect was so daunting that I began wondering whether one or the other of us was having second thoughts, if there was hesitation buried deep within the bureaucracy, secreted in the piles of paper and online forms that we were so keen to avoid.

And so it was entirely reasonable of Isabella to call me and ask what had become of Christopher. I've left three messages, she said, his mobile goes directly to voice mail, and the last time I rang it was a foreign ringtone—

She pronounced the word *foreign* with a familiar blend of suspicion, mystification (she could not imagine any reason why her only son would wish to remove himself from her vicinity) and pique. The words returned to me then, phrases spoken over the course of the marriage: you're foreign, you've always been a little foreign, she's very nice but different to us, we don't feel as if we know you (and then, finally, what she would surely say if Christopher told her that it was over between us), it's for the best, darling, in the end she was never really one of us.

—therefore, I would like to know, where exactly is my son?

Immediately, my head began to throb. It had been a month since I had spoken to Christopher. Our last conversation had been on the telephone. Christopher had said that although we were clearly not going to be reconciled, he did not want to begin the process—he used that word, indicative of some continuous and ongoing thing, rather than a decisive and singular act and of course he was right, divorce was more organic, somehow more contingent than it initially appeared—of telling people.

Could we keep it between us? I had hesitated, it wasn't that I disagreed with the sentiment—the decision was still new at that point, and I imagined Christopher felt much as I did, that we had not yet figured out how to tell the story of our separation. But I disliked the air of complicity, which felt incongruous and without purpose. Regardless, I said yes. Christopher, hearing the hesitation in my voice, asked me to promise. Promise that you won't tell anyone, at least for the time being, not until we speak again. Irritated, I agreed, and then hung up.

That was the last time we spoke. Now, when I insisted that I did not know where Christopher was, Isabella gave a short laugh before saying,

Don't be ridiculous. I spoke to Christopher three weeks ago and he told me the two of you were going to Greece. I've had such difficulty getting hold of him, and given that you are clearly here in England, I can only assume that he has gone to Greece without you.

I was too confused to respond. I could not understand why Christopher would have told her that we were going to Greece together, I had not even known that he was leaving the country. She continued, He's been working very hard, I know he's there on research, and—

She lowered her voice in a way that I found difficult to decipher, it might have been genuine hesitation or its mere facsimile, she was not above such manipulations.

—I'm worried about him.

This declaration was not immediately persuasive to me, and I did not take her concern with much seriousness. Isabella believed her relationship with Christopher to be better than it was, a natural mistake for a mother to make, but one that on occasion led to outlandish behavior on her part. Once, this situation might have elicited in me a feeling of triumph—that this woman should turn to me for help in a matter concerning her son might have meant something as little as a year ago, as little as six months ago.

Now, I listened mostly with trepidation as she continued. He hasn't been himself, I called to ask if the two of you—*the two of you* again, it was clear she knew nothing, that Christopher had not confided in her—might like to come and stay in the country, get some fresh air. That's when Christopher told me that you were going to Greece, that you had a translation to finish and that he was going to do research. But now—and she gave a brief sigh of exasperation—I find that you are in London and he is not answering his phone.

I don't know where Christopher is.

There was a slight pause before she continued.

In any case you must go and join him at once. You know how powerful my intuition is, I know something is wrong, it's not like him not to return my calls.

There were outcomes to Isabella's telephone call that are extraordinary to me, even now. One is that I obeyed this woman and went to Greece, a place I had no desire to visit, for a purpose that was not in the least bit evident to me. True, Christopher had lied to Isabella when he said that we were going to Greece together. If he did not want to tell his mother about the separation, it would have been easy enough to come up with some excuse to explain why he was traveling alone—that I had to go to a conference, that I was spending time with a girlfriend who had three children and was therefore always in need of both help and company.

Or he could have told her half the truth, the start of it at least, that we were taking time off—from what, or where, she might have asked. But he had not done any of this, perhaps because it was easier to lie or maybe because it was easier to let his mother make whatever assumptions she wished to make—although misapprehensions, after the fact, were especially difficult for Isabella. I realized then that we needed to formalize the state of affairs between us. I had already decided to ask Christopher for a divorce, I would simply go to Greece and do the deed in person.

I supposed it would be my last dutiful act as her daughter-in-law. An hour later, Isabella called to tell me which hotel Christopher was staying at—I wondered how she had obtained this information—and the record locator for a ticket she had booked in my name, departing the next day. Beneath the unnecessary flourishes of character and the sheen of idle elegance, she was a supremely capable woman, one reason why she had been a formidable adversary, someone I had reason to fear. But that was all over, and soon, there would be no battleground between us.

Still, I noted that she evidently didn't trust me—I was not the kind of wife who could be relied upon to locate her husband, not without a ticket in hand and a hotel address. Perhaps it was in response to this patent distrust that I kept my promise to Christopher, the second surprising outcome of Isabella's call. I did not tell his mother that we were separated, and had been for some time, the one piece of information that would have excused me from going to Greece altogether.

No mother would ask her daughter-in-law to go to Greece in order to ask her son for a divorce. I could have stayed in London and gone about my business. But I did not tell her, and I did not stay in London. If Isabella knew that she had purchased a plane ticket in order for me to ask her son for a divorce, I suppose she would have killed me, actually slain me then and there. Such a thing was not impossible. She was, as I have said, a supremely capable woman. Or perhaps she would have said had she known it was so easy to separate us, to dissolve the terms of our marriage, she would have bought me the ticket long ago. Before she hung up, she advised me to pack a bathing suit. She had been told the hotel had a very nice pool.

In Athens, the city was heavy with traffic and there was some kind of transportation strike. The village where Christopher was staying was a five-hour drive from the capital, at the southernmost tip of the country's mainland. A car was waiting at the airport: Isabella had thought of everything. I fell asleep during the journey, which began with the traffic, then segued into a series of bleak and anonymous motorways. I was tired. I looked out the window but could not read any of the signs.

I awoke to a hard and repetitive noise. It was black outside, night had fallen while I was asleep. The sound vibrated through the vehicle—*thwack thwack thwack*—then stopped. The car was moving slowly down a narrow single-lane road. I leaned forward and asked the driver if we were stopping, if we had very far to go. We are here, he said. We have already arrived. The thwacking began again.

Strays, the driver added. Outside, dark shapes moved alongside the car, the tails of the dogs hitting its shell. The driver beeped his horn in an effort to frighten the animals away—they were so close it seemed as if the car might strike them at any moment, despite our decelerated speed—but they were not deterred, they remained close to the vehicle as we moved down the road toward a large stone villa. The driver continued beeping his horn as he rolled down the window and shouted at the strays.

Up ahead, a porter opened the gates to the property. As the car moved forward through the gates, the dogs fell behind. When I turned to look through the rear window, they stood in a ring before the gates, their eyes as yellow as the beams from the taillights. The hotel was at the far end of a small bay and I heard the sound of water as soon as I stepped out of the car. I carried my purse and a small overnight bag, the porter asked if I had any luggage and I said I had none, I had packed for a night, at worst for a weekend, although I did not phrase it in that way.

The driver said something about a return journey; I took his card and said I would call him, perhaps tomorrow. He nodded, and I asked if he would now return to Athens, it was already very late. He shrugged and got back into the car.

Inside, the lobby was empty. I checked the time—it was nearly eleven. Isabella had not booked me a room, I was a woman joining her husband, there should have been no need. I asked for a single room for the night. The man behind the desk said there were plenty of rooms available, he announced with surprising candor that the hotel was nearly empty. It was the end of September, the season was over. Unfortunately, the sea was now too cold for swimming, he added, but the hotel swimming pool was heated to a very comfortable temperature.

I waited until he had finished taking my details and handed me the key before I asked about Christopher.

Would you like me to call his room?

His expression was alert but his hands remained still behind the desk, he did not move to pick up the phone, it was after all very late.

No, I shook my head. I'll try him in the morning.

The man nodded sympathetically. His eyes had become more watchful, perhaps he saw many relationships in similar disarray, or perhaps he thought nothing of it and had a naturally sympathetic face, a trait that was no doubt useful in his occupation. He did not say anything further about the matter. I took the key and he told me about breakfast and insisted on taking my bag as he ushered me to the elevator. Thank you, I said. Did I want a wake-up call? A newspaper in the morning? It can wait, I told him. All of it can wait.

When I woke, sunlight had flooded the room. I reached for my phone, there were no messages and it was already nine. Breakfast would be ending soon, I would need to hurry if I wanted to eat. Still, I stood in the shower longer than was necessary. Until that moment—standing in the hotel room shower, the water blurring my vision as it streamed into my eyes—I had not stopped to consider or imagine how Christopher would feel, what he would think, when he saw me, or was confronted by me, in the hotel. I imagined his first thought would be simple enough, he would assume that I wanted him back.

Why else would a woman follow her estranged husband to another country, other than to bring an end to their separation? It was an extravagant gesture, and extravagant gestures between a man and a woman are generally understood to be romantic, even in the context of a failed marriage. I would appear before him and he would—would he be filled with apprehension, would his heart sink, would he wonder what it was that I wanted? Would he feel caught, would he worry that there had been a disaster, that something had happened to his mother, he should have returned her phone calls?

Or would he be filled with hope, would he think that after all a reconciliation was in the cards (was this hope at the root of the promise he had extracted from me, and was it even a shared hope then, after all I had agreed to it), and would he then be disappointed, even more affronted than he might otherwise have been, by my petition for a divorce, which I nonetheless intended to make? I felt at once mortified for him and for myself, above all for the situation. I assumed—I had no prior experience to go on—that asking for a divorce was always discomfiting, but I could not believe it was always this awkward, the setting and the circumstances so ambiguous.

Downstairs, the lobby was empty. Breakfast was served on a terrace overlooking the sea. There was no sign of Christopher, the restaurant was also deserted. Below, the village was without shadow and so quiet as to be motionless, a collection of small buildings lined along a stone embankment. A large cliff formed one side of the bay, it was bare and without vegetation and cast a bright white light onto the water, the vista from the terrace was therefore both tranquil and dramatic. At the base of the cliff there were remnants of what looked like charred brush and grass, as if there had recently been a fire.

I drank my coffee. When he set down the cup, the waiter had informed me that the hotel was the only place where I would get my cappuccino, my latte, everywhere else it was Greek coffee or Nescafé. The setting here was romantic— Christopher liked luxurious accommodation, and luxury and romance were virtually synonyms for a certain class of people—and therefore made me uneasy. I imagined Christopher here, alone among a resort full of couples, it was the kind of hotel that was booked for honeymoons, for anniversaries. I felt another twinge of embarrassment, I wondered what he had been up to, the place was an absurdity.

I stopped the waiter when he brought my toast.

It's very quiet. Am I the last to come down for breakfast?

The hotel is empty. It is the off-season.

But there must be other guests.

The fires, he said, shrugging. They have discouraged people.

I don't know about the fires.

There have been wildfires all over the country. Fires all summer. The hills between here and Athens are black. If you go outside the village, up to the hills, you will see, the earth is still hot from the fire. It was in the newspapers. All around the

20

world. There were photographers—he mimed the click of a camera—all summer.

He tucked the tray under his arm and continued. They shot photographs for a fashion magazine here, at the hotel. The fire had spread to the cliff, you can still see the black—look. He gestured to the black-scarred surface of the rock. They put the models by the pool and the fire behind them and the sea—he sucked in his breath—it was very dramatic.

I nodded. He drifted away when I didn't say anything further. Unbidden, the image of Christopher in the midst of this photo shoot rose up. It was implausible, he stood between the models and the makeup artists and the stylist with a wry expression, as if he could not possibly begin to explain what he was doing in this circus. He looked even more like a stranger. I gazed around the terrace uneasily. It was nearing ten, evidently I had missed him at breakfast, he must have eaten early, perhaps he had already left the hotel for the day.

I rose and went into the lobby. The man who had checked me in the night before had been replaced by a young woman with heavy features, she wore her hair scraped back in a manner that did not suit her, the style was too severe for her soft, full face. I asked her if Christopher had been down that morning. She frowned, I sensed that she did not want to tell me. I asked if she

21

could call his room. She kept her eyes on my face as she dialed the number, I listened to the pulse of the bell, beneath her professional hairline, her expression was openly sullen.

She hung up.

He's not in his room. Would you like to leave a message?

I need to speak with him urgently.

Who are you?

The question was blunt, almost hostile.

I'm his wife.

She looked startled, at once I understood—Christopher was a careless flirt, he did it without thinking, as a reflex, the way people said *hello, thank you, you're welcome,* the way a man held open a door for a woman. He was too liberal in this regard, he risked spreading his charm thin. Once you perceived the patches where it had worn through, it was hard to see the charm—hard to see the man himself, if you were in any way wary of charisma—entirely whole again. But most people did not stay in his orbit long enough for this to happen, most people were like this young girl, I could see that she was protective of him, still in his thrall.

Him, Him, as if he belonged to her. I stepped back from the counter.

Please tell him that his wife is looking for him.

She nodded.

As soon as he returns. It's important.

She muttered something below her breath as I left, cursing me no doubt. The wife is always the subject of cursing, never more so than in such a situation.

I'd like to go for a walk.

She looked up, she could not believe that I was still there, she was waiting for me to leave, my presence was clearly unpleasant to her. But I found myself lingering, it was true that I wanted to go for a walk and I did not know where to go. She gave me directions to the quay, she said the village was small and I would not get lost. I nodded and went outside. Although it was September it was still hot and the light was very bright. For a moment I was almost blinded, I thought I could smell the faint whiff of char in the air, as if the land was still burning: a moment of synesthesia.

Almost as soon as I stepped past the hotel gates, the stray dogs appeared. They approached me with their tails fanning through the air in a manner that was neither friendly nor hostile. I liked dogs. I would have even gotten a dog, once upon a time, but Christopher was against it, he said we traveled too much, which was true. I reached out to touch the nearest dog. His hair was thin and short, the surface so sleek that it was more like touching skin than fur. His right eye was milky with blindness but the gaze was both intelligent and desolate, its animal blankness unmitigated.

The other dogs writhed around me, their bodies momentarily rubbing against my sides, my hands and fingers, before falling away. They accompanied me as I made my way down to the embankment, running forward and then circling back again in a slow spiral of movement. Only the dog with the milky eye remained fixed at my side. It was nearing noon. The water in the bay was clear and blue. A few solitary boats dotted its surface.

Gerolimenas was a small fishing village, I came upon a handful of shops—a newsstand, a tobacconist, a pharmacy—all of which were shuttered. As I walked and the dogs eventually dispersed, I looked for Christopher among the scant faces seated outside the taverna, most of which were lined and well weathered, much darkened by the sun. They bore nothing in common with Christopher's smooth and pampered countenance, which would have stood out in contrast. He had been attractive—to women, to people in general—his entire life and that could not help but have an effect.

Nor was Christopher to be found among the figures on the embankment, idle men and women, a couple of fishermen. The small beach itself was empty. I stood by the water and looked back at the hotel, which had become entirely incongruous in the ten minutes it had taken to walk here. Within the grounds of the hotel you could have been anywhere, luxury was by and large anonymous, but once you passed beyond its carefully guarded confines, you were forcibly in this particular setting and place. I was aware that the villagers were watching me—it was their right, I was the intruder here—and I lowered my head and retreated in the direction of the hotel.

When I returned, less than an hour had passed. In the lobby, I saw that the young woman had disappeared and the man from the previous evening had returned. He looked up, then stepped from behind his desk and hurried in my direction.

I'm sorry to bother you—

What is it?

My colleague has told me that you are the wife of Mr. Wallace.

Yes?

Your husband was due to check out this morning. But he has not checked out.

I looked at my watch.

It's only just noon.

The fact is, we have not seen him for several days. He went on a trip, and hasn't returned.

I shook my head.

Where has he gone?

He hired a car, a driver, but that is all we know. He had already paid for the room in advance, he said that he would keep it while he was gone.

For a long moment, we stared at each other in silence. Then the man cleared his throat, politely.

You see, his room is needed.

Excuse me?

The persons who have reserved that room are arriving today.

But the hotel is empty.

He shrugged apologetically.

Yes, I know. But people are absurd. A wedding anniversary, I think. The room has special meaning to them, they passed their honeymoon in it. They are due to arrive in the afternoon, and so you see . . .

He trailed off.

We would like to move his belongings from one room to another.

That seems reasonable.

Or perhaps we should pack them up, if he intends to leave with you today?

I don't know how long he plans to stay.

Yes, I see.

He is doing research.

The man held his hands up, as if I had said something unnecessary.

We will need to begin packing his room now. Perhaps you could accompany me?

I waited as he returned to the desk to retrieve a key. Together, we walked to Christopher's room, which was located at the opposite end of the hotel, on the top floor, the man—whose name was Kostas, according to the badge that was pinned to his jacket—explained to me that Christopher had been staying in a suite. The room had wonderful views of the bay, should I decide to extend my stay, he could recommend it wholeheartedly, it would become available once the honeymoon couple left, perhaps by that point my husband would have returned.

When we reached the room at last, Kostas knocked on the door with the discreet but somehow still peremptory gesture common to hotel staff, his hand already on the knob—for a moment, I hallucinated a vision of the door opening and Christopher standing before us, surprised but not entirely displeased—and then Kostas unlocked the door and we entered.

The room was unrecognizable to me. Christopher was not fastidious by any means, but he was not slovenly and he rarely inhabited a space that was not clean (it was not that he tidied the space himself, he had people who did that for him—the cleaning lady, for a time it had been me). The room—although large, with a separate sitting area and a remarkable view, Kostas was right, it was an excellent room and must have been one of the more expensive at the hotel—was entirely disordered.

The floor was strewn with discarded clothes, at least several days' worth, the desk was covered in books and papers, by the side of the bed there was a tangle of electrical cords, headphones, a camera, his laptop lay on the floor with the lid open at an oblique angle. There were remnants of room service trays, pots of coffee and half-empty bottles of water, even a plate covered in crumbs— I could not understand why the maid had not at least taken away the dirty dishes. Meanwhile the bed sat in the center of the room, unmade and covered in newspapers and notebooks.

The surfaces had been wiped and the floor vacuumed but it was almost as though the maid had worked around the mess, in order to preserve it. He told the maid not to touch anything, Kostas said. He shrugged. People make requests, we just follow orders. But you see—

He stepped to the wardrobe and opened the doors. More soiled laundry lay on the floor inside. Above, a selection of shirts and trousers, all of which I recognized—the patterns and fabrics, the minutely frayed hem on one of the cuffs. The sensation of being in the room remained one of severe dissociation and yet here—and here—and here—in these objects, which I had lived with for many years, there was a stab of recognition, the recollection of the owner, the man, who was here and also not here.

Kostas clapped his hands together.

So. We'll pack it up? This is fine with you?

I nodded as I looked down at the papers and books. They were uniformly about Greece, there was even a Greek phrase book among them. I opened a notebook, but I could not decipher

Christopher's tight, messy script. I had never been able to read it. Kostas used the room phone to call the front desk and request a chambermaid, who appeared several minutes later and began packing the clothes. He apologized, but it was now nearly one, the new guests would be arriving at any moment and I could see there was a great deal to be done before the room would be ready.

My phone was ringing. I reached inside my pocket. It was Isabella, she had impeccable timing. I answered, a little short, but she didn't notice, she didn't even bother to say hello before she asked where Christopher was and if she could speak to him.

I could hear a recording of Britten's *Billy Budd* playing in the background. Isabella and Mark were opera fanatics and had once taken us to see a production of this particular opera at Glyndebourne. It had been an unhappy expedition. By that point, the cracks in our marriage were beginning to show. Christopher and I were barely on speaking terms, but Isabella and Mark were blithely, almost aggressively unaware of the tension between us. There was something single-minded about their interest in opera, and never more so than on that evening.

I remembered sitting in the theater in a state of numbed contemplation—of the music, the awkwardness of the situation, I was not a fan of Britten, which did nothing to endear me to

Christopher's parents. Now, as I heard the familiar strains of music, I thought how integral distance was to the story, which takes place almost entirely at sea. Without that distance, even the basic mechanics of the plot would be impossible—no threat of mutiny, no reliance on martial law, no death of Billy Budd. If I did not care for the opera—the music was too dense, like staring at a stone wall—the story was still compelling, it offered the opportunity to peer into the world of men, in a different time, when men went away, to war or to sea.

Now, they no longer went away—there was not, at least for most of them, a sea to roam or a desert to cross, there was nothing but the floors of an office tower, the morning commute, a familiar and monotonous landscape, in which life became something secondhand, not something a man could own for himself. It was only on the shores of infidelity that they achieved a little privacy, a little inner life, it was only in the domain of their faithlessness that they became, once again, strangers to their wives, capable of anything.

Abruptly, the music cut off and Isabella repeated her question, Where is Christopher? After a brief pause as I stared at the room's wreckage, I told her that I hadn't found him. But you are there? You are in Mani? Yes. But Christopher isn't here, he isn't at the hotel. Then where is he? I don't know, I said. He's taken a trip somewhere, he hired a driver. His phone isn't ringing, probably he left his charger—as I spoke, my eyes fell on the device's cord, hanging limp in the socket by the bed—here at the hotel.

I'll wait, I told her. You won't come back until you find him, she said. You must find him. I will, I said. But I'm not sure I am the person who should be looking for him.

If she had listened, if she had stopped to ask what I meant, I would have told her, standing in this hotel room, the secret of our separation no longer felt valid—but she did not pause or even appear to hear me. You won't come back until you find him, she repeated, you must bring him back. She sounded unhinged, it was essentially a terrible relationship. It was no wonder Christopher had been running away from her the whole of his life, or since he had become an adult man—he was always running away before he was running toward anything.

I lowered the phone. I told Kostas that they could pack the rest of Christopher's things into his cases and when he returned he could tell them what to do himself. Kostas nodded and then I turned and left the room. I was free to go.

2.

But I did not leave. I told Kostas that I would stay another day or two, it was very pleasant at the hotel. To sit and do nothing in the perfect weather. I had my lunch outside and then I swam in the swimming pool, which was as warm as Kostas had promised, more like an enormous bath than a swimming pool. Isabella had been correctly informed, it was a very nice pool. I read a little, I had some work to do but nothing very taxing, nothing that was urgent.

And I did not mind this delay, this waiting, which on the face of it did not look like hesitation. But until a decision is acted upon, it is only hypothetical, a kind of thought experiment: I had decided to ask Christopher for a divorce but I had not yet committed the act, I had not looked at him and spoken the words. It was important, this act of enunciation, these words, or rather this| one word—*divorce*—which thus far had been notably absent from our conversation, and which, once spoken, would change the course of our separation inalterably.

Of course it had been in the air—as the endgame, the worst-case scenario, an inevitability or relief. The word was weighted, *ça me pèse*, a condition of adulthood. In childhood, words are weightless—

I shout *I hate you* and it means nothing, the same can be said for *I love you*—but as an adult, those very words are used with greater care, they no longer slip out of the mouth with the same ease. *I do* is another example, a phrase that in childhood is only the stuff of playacting, a game between children, but then grows freighted with meaning.

How many times had I myself spoken these words? Only once since becoming an adult. Christopher and I were married in a courtroom and arrived only minutes before the brief ceremony, there was no rehearsal, the judge assured us that we need only repeat after him, even an idiot couldn't get it wrong. And so when I said *I do* before the assembled group of our family and friends, it was for the first time, or at least the first time since childhood.

I remembered being surprised by the power of the ritual, the ceremonial act of speaking these words, which took on a deep and almost maniac significance. It suddenly made sense that these words—*I do*—would be paired with the archaic and unreasonable phrase *until death do us part,* which was morbid and apparently out of place in what was meant to be a joyful occasion, but which nonetheless served a clear purpose: to remind the participants of the crazed wager they were making in this act, this act being marriage.

I tried to remember what else I had felt during the ceremony, not so many years ago but long enough for my memory to be uncertain. I thought there had been a brief moment of terror but mostly I had been happy, I had been very happy, for a long time it was a good and optimistic marriage. For all these reasons, it was difficult to contemplate the pronouncement of the word that would destroy all that optimism, however outdated—and so although I remained at the hotel in order to ask Christopher for a divorce, I found that I was in no hurry to confront him, I had made a decision that I believed to be absolute, and yet I could have sat in the sun for days, for weeks, without moving, without doing anything, without speaking a word.

Later that afternoon, a couple arrived who could only have been the pair that was to occupy Christopher's room. They stumbled through the lobby already drunk, they must have begun in the car, the same driver who had delivered me to the hotel followed them into the lobby dragging three large cases behind him. Briefly, his eyes met mine, but apart from a small nod he did not acknowledge me, he had his hands full with the couple.

They looked Scandinavian, both pale and blue-eyed and essentially incongruous in this landscape, for which they had not been designed. The woman's hair was bleached blond and the man was somehow already sunburnt, his skin a hectic and uncomfortable red. They were evidently very fond of each other. They kissed constantly, even from across the lobby I could see how they were flexing their tongues in an impressively muscular fashion, they could not give Kostas—he was on duty behind the desk, his face stoic—more than a single piece of information—their name, their country of origin, their date of departure—before they were at it again.

Kostas stared at the wall behind the embracing couple as he told them that breakfast was served on the terrace, asked which newspaper they wanted in the morning, whether they would be needing a wake-up call, although it was obvious they would not. The pair seemed undeterred by the utter quiet of the hotel. When they spoke they were overloud and giddy, they allowed their voices to carry, it was as if they believed themselves to be checking into a hotel in Las Vegas or Monaco.

I watched as they followed Kostas across the lobby, arms wrapped around each other, it was remarkable how constantly they telegraphed their desire for each other, it simply did not let up. They disappeared up the stairs and in the direction of Christopher's room, although of course it was no longer Christopher's room, the porter following with their bags. Earlier that afternoon I had seen the same porter carrying Christopher's cases, one in each hand, down rather than up the stone staircase, to the lobby storage room.

Of Christopher himself there had been no sign.

I sat on the terrace for the remainder of the afternoon with a novel I was considering translating, about a couple whose child goes missing in the desert. The novel had been sent to me by a publisher, I would need to translate a sample chapter at least, we would need to see if it was a good fit. The task of a translator is a strange one. People are prone to saying that a successful translation doesn't feel like a translation at all, as if the translator's ultimate task is to be invisible.

Perhaps that is true. Translation is not unlike an act of channeling, you write and you do not write the words. Christopher always found the way I spoke about my work too vague, it did not impress him, perhaps because he thought it was imprecise and even mystical, or perhaps because he intuited what I was really saying, which was that translation's potential for passivity appealed to me. I could have been a translator or a medium, either would have been the perfect occupation for me. Such a statement would of course have horrified him, and been crafted to do so. Christopher had wanted to be a writer—not just a writer, but an author—since he was a child.

I continued reading for several hours. Once or twice I saw Kostas, he brought me a coffee, asked if I planned to dine in the hotel that evening. He made no mention of Christopher, and the one time I asked if he had returned, Kostas shook his head and shrugged. No sign of him, nothing at all. In the evening, the young woman who had been on duty that morning returned, giving me a sour look as she passed through the lobby.

I watched her as she went on her way, although the hotel was quiet she apparently had a great many things to do, she was constantly rushing from one side of the lobby to the other, answering the phone, barking orders to the porters and maids. She was not unattractive, I tried to imagine Christopher and this woman together—he would have flirted with her at the very least, perhaps he had even gone to bed with her, such a thing was not impossible, or even unlikely.

As I continued observing her, I could see that although she was not pretty—her features were too heavy to be described in such conventional terms, they were very expressive, which was generally not considered appealing in a woman's face (hence the mania for treatments like Botox, for face creams that promised to freeze the features into youthful immobility; it was more than the mere pursuit of youth, it arose out of a universal aversion to a woman's propensity to be excessive, to be *too much*)—she was alluring, undoubtedly so.

She had the kind of body that intrigued men. They looked at it and wondered what it would be like to touch, how its contours would feel beneath their hands, what was its weight and heft. I noted that, with her heavy brow and long black hair—

plaited in a simple braid that hung halfway down her back—she was my physical opposite. It was more than a question of coloring, she had a supremely practical body, one whose purpose was clear. The purposes of my own body were sometimes too opaque, there had been many moments when its discrete parts—legs, arms, torso—made no sense even to me, as they lay there on the bed.

But this woman's body made sense. I watched her through the glass as she moved back and forth across the lobby, she was wearing a hotel uniform and was shod in sensible shoes, it was the kind of job that kept you on your feet all day long. Although she walked quickly, it was as if her body were leaden, she was a woman firmly tethered to the ground. Perhaps such carnality was in the end irresistible. Christopher would have perceived her allure at once, he was a sophisticated man, whose marriage was suspended, also a man with no scruples and a tourist in this place, everything around him would have appeared essentially disposable.

And she would have been susceptible to Christopher's charm—he was handsome and wealthy, alone and unencumbered, evidently idle (only an idle man could stay in this hotel and village for so long, most visitors stayed for a few days, a weekend, most people came for a holiday). I sat on the terrace, the sun beating down on my face. The images came easily, I knew the ways of one half of the coupling, and it took very little imagination to see the rest. I could remember—with a dispassionate eye, it had happened a long time ago—Christopher's way of approaching a woman, of entering her consciousness, he was very good at impressing himself upon a person.

I ordered a drink. It was hot, sweat pooled in the crevice of my collarbone. He grasped her wrist, pressing first his thumb and then his forefinger against her skin. She looked up, not at him, but to see if anyone was watching. The lobby was empty, there was nothing to worry about. The waiter brought my drink. Would I be needing anything else? No, I was fine. Let me adjust the umbrella, the sun is very hot. Before I could stop him he had dragged the heavy stand several feet, the base made a loud scraping sound against the stone floor.

The waiter gripped the edge of the umbrella and tilted it over my face. It was better, there was shade, it was true that the sun was too bright, and I thanked him. He led her by the hand, she walked behind him but urged him to move quickly, the shame if they were caught. The waiter did not move away. There's nothing to worry about, he said. In that moment, she chose to believe him. She followed him up to his room. They were still on the hotel premises, there was nowhere else to go, she would have died rather than bring him back to her house, with her mother and father sleeping in the room next door and her brother and sisters, all of them living in the same house.

I'm fine, I said. Thank you again. He opened the door, he stepped aside and let her enter first. The waiter's silhouette blocked out the sun. There is nothing else I can get for you? he said, almost wistfully. Inside the room it was cool, the windows had been left open and the door to the balcony was ajar, she tensed—suppose one of the maids was in the room, it was unlikely at this hour but possible—he dropped the room key onto the table, he checked his phone for messages, he was relaxed in a way that seemed miraculous to her, she could not imagine being so at ease in this luxurious room.

No, thank you, really I am fine. At last he moved away. She thought he would offer her a drink—wasn't that what was supposed to happen? She didn't know, she had never been in this situation before, he could have called for room service, a bottle of champagne like the ones she had seen sent up to so many rooms, so many couples—but he put down his phone and then he turned and seized her by the shoulder without preamble, so that she was at once affronted and excited. Had it been this way? Almost certainly. I closed my eyes. It was a long time ago but I remembered it well enough, it would not have been very different, with this woman or another.

And then the rest, the same as well. She would have been pleased by the end of it, almost certainly, and there might have been as long as ten minutes or even half an hour before the doubt began. What happened now? He was not asleep (he never fell asleep in that moment, but she would not know that), he was not looking at her, he was simply staring at the ceiling. She hesitated, she had drifted off—for how long? She could hardly ask him—tentatively, she placed her hand on his arm. Hardly a touch at all, but he turned, smiled, covered her hand with his.

I had dinner early. Once again, the terrace was deserted. The restaurant had been set for the dinner service, there were now white tablecloths on every table, flowers and even candles. There was a German family with two young children, who ate quickly and left shortly after I arrived. The children were very solemn, very well behaved. They sat mostly in silence, the mother occasionally leaning forward to cut the boy's food. I recognized the waiters from breakfast, once the family departed they quickly cleared the table and set it afresh, as if the restaurant were fully booked for the evening, and then they were idle again.

As I was ordering my coffee, the honeymoon couple arrived. That was how I had come to think of them, although Kostas had said they had come to Gerolimenas to celebrate their anniversary, they behaved in every way like newlyweds. They were still drunk, or had become even more drunk, since their arrival that afternoon. Upon entering the restaurant they began exclaiming enthusiastically at the view, the woman clutching at the man's elbow, it was true that the vista was spectacular, the sun was setting and the sky was a vivid smear of color.

They sat down to their dinner. The man immediately ordered champagne. They were celebrating, why not? Everything *why not,* they repeated the phrase again and again, tossing it back and forth as if it were a ball. They ordered lobster, why not, caviar, why not, they spoke in English to the waiter, gesticulating wildly, at one point the woman actually waved her menu through the air. The waiter brought their champagne, a basket of bread, glasses of ice water.

I asked for the bill and signed it to the room. It was early and I did not want to spend the rest of the evening in my room, so I walked along the stone jetty that ran from the terrace out into the water. It was a solid and impressive construction, perhaps ten feet wide and stretching out some hundred feet into the sea, far enough for the water to feel enveloping. Soon the persistent clatter of the restaurant, even the noise of the honeymoon couple, had been absorbed by the darkness.

And then nothing but the sound of the water. I

reached the end of the jetty and sat down on its edge. In another life, Christopher and I might have been like the quiet family, or even the honeymoon couple, they were possibilities that had never come to fruition, and only because of that been rendered absurd. I heard footsteps behind me. The waiter appeared, bearing a glass of wine, compliments of the hotel, he said. Perhaps I looked as if I needed it. I asked if the tide was rising and he said yes, at high tide the water nearly reached the top of the jetty. I asked him if people ever drowned in the water.

Yes, sometimes. But the water is safe. There are no whirlpools. No sharks.

I looked up to see if he was smiling but his expression wasn't visible in the dark.

Most of the people who drowned were suicides.

The statement had the air of a joke.

Were there so many?

He shook his head, he was backing away, he seemed almost affronted.

Hardly any.

He retreated and I called out after him, I said I would be along in a moment, in the event that he was worried. He nodded and then went back inside. I rose several moments later, as I stood in the darkness, the glass door on a small balcony on the third floor of the hotel opened. The honeymoon couple emerged. They were embracing passionately and did not stop to look out at the water, or lean on the edge of the rail and light a cigarette, any of the things one usually steps out onto a balcony to do. The man was running his hand up and down the woman's back and she was gripping his jaw with one hand as she slipped the other down the back of his trousers.

I was embarrassed—it was unpleasant to be standing in the dark like a Peeping Tom, I didn't know where to look, almost everything around me was dark, while up above the embracing couple was brilliantly illuminated, as if they were standing on a stage. There was nothing elegant or even erotic in the sight of them, their passion was grotesque. They continued grinding up against each other with animal passion, it was clear that however much of a performance they made of their desire for each other, it was nonetheless the real thing.

It was the real thing, and yet I was certain they were aware of how dramatically the light fell on them, how the balcony was framed against the night. Having paid a premium for the suite, for this hotel, so evidently designed for romance, they would have been aware of its theatrical possibilities. Every romance requires a backdrop and an audience, even—or perhaps especially— the genuine ones, romance is not something that a couple can be expected to conjure by themselves, you and another, the two of you together, not just once but again and again, love in general is fortified by its context, nourished by the gaze of others.

As for this particular context, I thought, it had also been Christopher's room, and he must have stood on the balcony himself, in the very place where the passionate couple now stood, alone or perhaps with someone else. I remained at the end of the jetty a moment longer and watched the couple's long embrace, I watched until at last she took him by the hand and led him into the bedroom, closing the door behind them. Then I walked back to the terrace and into the lobby. The young woman was behind the desk. I nodded to her as I entered the lobby, she raised her eyes and then called to me.

Have you heard from him?

I stopped. When I turned, she was looking down at the floor, it was as if she had been unable to keep herself from asking the question and now regretted it. Then she raised her eyes defiantly and looked directly at me with her frank gaze. We had nothing in common, there was nothing between us. And yet I was certain that we were both waiting for the same man, her question only furthered the belief. I shook my head. She looked both disappointed and relieved, I understood at once that it would have been a blow to her if I had said yes, that I was going to meet him, that he was upstairs in my room at that very moment.

He'll turn up, I said. She nodded. Has he done

this before? Is this what he is like? Essentially unreliable? Does he simply disappear, without a word? The questions as clear as if she had spoken them. I did not want to comfort her for troubles that were not my own, that it was not my business to know. But for some reason I continued, although she was silent, I felt as though I needed to say something. Lately, he has not been himself. She flinched, I saw that the words were disagreeable to her, perhaps she thought I intended to imply that the encounter—whatever it might have been, if there had been one at all— was out of character, weightless, a meaningless aberration.

He has not been himself. She had become sullen again. A flash of anger darkened her features. It was possible that for once Christopher had bitten off more than he could chew, that she was more than he'd bargained for. Perhaps he had fled this woman, perhaps that was the reason for his absence—but then why leave his belongings behind, why not simply depart or change hotels, there were any number of establishments in the area that would have served just as well. And Christopher, in the way of serial womanizers, never had difficulty shaking off a woman.

After a moment, I asked her what her name was and she hesitated and then told me, Maria. It is nice to meet you, I said, and when she did nothing more than give another curt nod, her eyes averted, I turned and left. I thought to myself as I went that I had bungled the encounter somehow. But how could I have known that she would be so emotional? I felt a surge of relief, I did not envy her the tumult of feeling, the jealousy and uncertainty, she evidently did not know whether to feel outraged or ashamed. And despite everything, she remained hopeful, I could see it in her face. It was a terrible thing, to love and not know whether you were loved in return, it led to the worst sensations—jealousy, rage, self-loathing—to all these lesser states.

3.

I called Isabella the following morning and told her that I had not found Christopher, that he had not yet returned to the hotel. She asked me if I was not worried. I told her that I wasn't. Christopher had come to Greece to do research, he might easily have arranged a short trip to a neighboring village, or returned to Athens to consult some archives. Research! She laughed. What kind of research?

Christopher had published his first book when he was still in his twenties, and it had been received with great enthusiasm by the publishing world and also the general public, briefly appearing at the bottom of the bestseller list. It had been an unusual book, even idiosyncratic, a work of nonfiction about the social life of music—its role in rituals and ceremonies, the way it demarcated public space, its function as a form of religious and ideological persuasion.

The book was wide-ranging and digressive, and the writing had much of Christopher's personal charm. One moment he was comparing the relative intimacy of chamber music to the pomp of orchestral music, the next he was detailing his experience as a teenager frequenting various London nightclubs. He wrote about the music of the Third Reich, about the acoustics at the Gewandhaus, he went to King's College chapel to listen to Handel's cantatas (he had attended King's as an undergraduate, I assumed the act, accompanied by the music and then the writing, was a recuperation of sorts).

True, the book was not especially well researched—the few critical reviews had pointed out some glaring errors and elisions, but by and large these dissenting voices could be comfortably categorized as such. After all, he was not an academic and the book had been written for a general readership. Christopher himself was something of a generalist. What he was good at— what the book had achieved with impressive and seeming ease—was drawing connections between an array of disparate sources, and making the material cohere in the prose.

I didn't know Christopher at the time of the book's publication. When I met him he was occupying the relatively comfortable life that is made available to relatively successful authors. He was invited to give lectures, to write reviews for various newspapers, his book had been translated into several languages. He was offered a teaching position at some university, which he declined—he didn't need the money, he was writing a second book, which was under contract to his publisher, and which he was already late in delivering.

He was working on it when we met. A procrastinator, he was prone to talking about the project at length, almost making a little performance of it, and I soon realized that he preferred talking about the book to writing it. He described it as a study of mourning rituals around the world, a work of cultural and political science that would encompass both secular and religious ceremonies, delineating—I think that was the word he used—a landscape of cultural and historical difference.

It was a strange project for a man who had hitherto lost nothing of significance, whose life was intact in all its key particulars. If he had cause for grief, it was only in the abstract. But he was drawn to people who were in a state of loss. This gave people the mistaken impression that he was a sympathetic man. His sympathy lasted as long as his curiosity, once that had gone he suddenly withdrew, making himself unavailable, or at least less available than people might reasonably have expected, given the sudden and violent intimacy he had forced upon them in the first place.

But that was his manner, his way of being. He was a gifted writer but something of a dilettante in his approach to his career—in the five years we had been married, I had never known him to go to a library, even during the extended periods when he was preoccupied with his research. No doubt this was why Isabella sneered at his work;

despite its relative success, she did not take it seriously, she would have preferred for him to have a career in law, finance, even politics, she liked to say that he had the wiles and charisma for it.

Still, as I have said, Christopher could speak on his subject with great authority. And although there is nothing essentially frivolous about mourning, he was able to talk about particular rituals and traditions in a manner that was wholly entertaining, his own interest in the subject matter was infectious. Christopher had almost certainly come to Greece in order to study its professional mourners, the women who were paid to issue lamentations at funerals. I had known this the moment Isabella told me he had gone to Greece, it was a matter of considerable interest to him, and was going to figure strongly in the book he was writing.

The ancient practice, he had explained to me, was rapidly dying out. There were only a few parts of rural Greece where it was still practiced, the southern Peloponnese, a region called Mani, was one of them. There, every village had a few mourners—weepers or wailers, as they were sometimes called—women who performed the funeral dirge at a village burial. What intrigued him about the practice was its externalization of grief: the fact that a body other than the body of the bereaved expressed its woe.

Literally an out-of-body experience, he had said. You, the bereaved, are completely liberated from the need to emote. All the pressures of the funeral, the expectation that you will perform your grief for the assembled crowd—imagine that you are a widow, burying your husband, people expect a good show. But the nature of grief is incompatible with this demand, people say that when you are grieving, when you have experienced a profound loss, you are impaled beneath it, hardly in a condition to express your sorrow.

Instead, you purchase an instrument to express your sorrow, or perhaps it's less like an instrument and more like a tape recorder and tape, you simply press play and the ceremony, the long and elaborate production, carries on without you. You walk away and are left alone with your grief. It is a remarkably enlightened arrangement, of course the financial aspect is crucial, the fact that it is a monetary transaction makes the entire arrange-ment clean, refined. It's no wonder that such a custom is native to Greece, the so-called cradle of civilization—it makes perfect sense.

He was half joking, I remember that he was actually laughing as he spoke. For a moment I was startled. It was as if the man standing before me was splitting in two—on the one hand he spoke like a man who had never lost anything, not a wife or a lover or a parent, not even a pet dog, a man who had no conception of what real loss must feel like. And I knew this to be the case from a factual point of view, I knew the man's history. But at the same time, I thought I could perceive the shadow of a man who had lost something or someone very dear to him, even a man who had at one point lost everything, in his voice—ironic and cool with distance—there was the intimation of some unseen depth.

But what such a loss could be—this escaped me. I asked him once why he was writing the book, it was more than a question of interest—the writing of a book cannot, in my experience, be sustained by simple interest, it requires something more, it is generally the work of years, after all. But he did not reply, not at once and then not at all, he merely shook his head and turned away, as if the answer was mysterious even to himself. He had spoken about the book with increasing frequency over the past year, it came up again and again in conversation, as if the unfinished volume weighed on him, and yet he could not explain his reasons for writing it.

That was why, no doubt, he was unable to finish the book. Christopher was a charming man, and charm is made up of surfaces—every charming man is a confidence man. But not even that is the point. What I am talking about are the natural failures of a relationship, even one that for a time had been very good. In the end, what is a relationship but two people, and between two people there will always be room for surprises and misapprehensions, things that cannot be explained. Perhaps another way of putting it is that between two people, there will always be room for failures of imagination.

As soon as I hung up the phone, it rang again. It was Yvan. I had called him from the airport in Athens but it had been a rushed conversation—I was looking for the driver, the arrivals terminal was chaotic, the tannoy making a constant stream of announcements in both English and Greek—and we had not spoken since. The time difference between England and Greece was minimal but the journey was long, causing a palpable lag in our communication, some kind of delay between us.

He asked how the journey had been, how I had found Christopher—he hesitated before he asked after Christopher, and I said at once that he was not here. That in fact he was nowhere to be ound. Yvan was silent, and then said, What do you mean he's not there, was Isabella wrong? It's not like Isabella to be wrong. I said, No, she wasn't wrong. He was here, but he's not here at the moment, I'm waiting for him to return. Then Yvan was silent for a moment longer, before asking, How long will you wait?

I said, It makes sense to wait, doesn't it? And

after yet another pause, Yvan said, Yes, it makes sense. But I don't like the idea of you there alone, I'm not going to lie, it makes me nervous. This was unusually blunt for Yvan, he was not the kind of man who liked to make demands. Even as he spoke his voice was mild, there was not a hint of reproach. There's nothing to be nervous about but I understand, I said, it's an awkward situation. Then Yvan said, Why don't I come out and join you?

When I ran into Yvan three months ago—in the street, literally in the middle of a crossing—he suggested that we go into the coffee shop on the corner rather than stand in the cold. Even now, with the benefit of hindsight, I can't say for certain that he made the invitation with anything in mind apart from the wind and light rain. Neither of us was dressed for the weather, the temperature had dropped out of nowhere, he said, in exactly the same tone he used to ask if he shouldn't join me in Gerolimenas.

At any rate, I accepted the invitation. I had always liked Yvan, he was handsome but in a manner that was unassuming, there was nothing demanding about his good looks. In this sense he was different from Christopher, who was aware of his appearance and knew too well how to exploit its effect—toward the end of our marriage, only at the very tail end, it became clear to me that he knew the angles from which he appeared most distinguished, and that over time he had perfected a series of appealing looks, glances, expressions and gestures, a trait that was absurd and essentially unlovable.

Yvan was better-looking than Christopher, but almost certainly did not give that impression, you had to look quite hard to discern the handsome man behind the shambling exterior. I had never thought of him as handsome. And yet as we sat across the table from each other and he inquired, in his very kind manner, as to the facts of my life and how I was doing, it was evident that it was because I found him attractive that I told him, rather abruptly and in confidence, that Christopher and I had separated. He was the first person I told.

This was before Christopher had extracted from me the promise not to tell anyone about the separation. If Yvan was surprised, he didn't show it, he only said that he was very sorry, that we had always seemed happy together, we had been one of the couples he had enjoyed spending time with. Then he laughed in a self-conscious way, he didn't mean to speak about himself, regarding a matter that had nothing to do with him—but then, of course, it ended up having everything to do with him, his words presaged the arrangement that would follow, for which he did and would continue to feel guilty, perhaps he had a sense of it even then.

Yvan was a journalist and a friend of Christopher's first, they had known each other very slightly at university. Christopher—Yvan later told me, Christopher and I had never spoken of Yvan as anything other than a present-day acquaintance, although I was aware that they had been at Cambridge together, I suspected that Christopher had only the vaguest memory of Yvan from those days, he was a born amnesiac— had been charismatic, a prominent figure on campus, one of those students of whom the entire student body is aware.

This was entirely in keeping with what I knew about Christopher, what was then more revealing was the manner in which Yvan described Christopher, as though he were recounting the experience of seeing an actor on a stage, observed not from the audience but from the wings. Yvan was in some ways still the same man, essentially shy, preferring to be on the margins rather than in the center of things. And yet he had been drawn into Christopher's orbit, Yvan told me that for a time, Christopher had made a concerted effort to befriend him.

He hesitated a little before he told the story, perhaps he thought that it might not be in the best taste, it was early in what was to become our relationship and it was a strange intimacy to assert, a reminder of the fact that the two men had known each other before either had known me, that Yvan would always know this youthful version of Christopher better than I could. Experience accumulated in haphazard places, the wrong bits of knowledge residing with the wrong parties. But I insisted, I was amused and a little intrigued, I hardly needed to be protected from Christopher, whether in his old or current incarnations.

Although by Yvan's own account he was not a popular student on campus—he did not come from good family, or display unusual wealth, nor was he exceptional in any obvious way, he did not possess charm or style or wit in externalized form—Christopher had pursued his friendship with the intensity that is particular to collegiate relationships, often between men, but also women. Perhaps he did so because he sensed that Yvan naturally possessed the one quality that Christopher respected, but lacked the discipline to truly seek out and embrace: that is, a genuine indifference to his charm.

Gradually, as Yvan described their brief friendship, I grew uncomfortable, disliking the versions of both men that emerged—Christopher's manic charisma and compulsion to seduce, Yvan's inexplicable passivity, neither accepting nor rebuffing Christopher's advances. Yvan felt my discomfort, his suspicions had been correct, the intimacy between the two men was off-putting to me. There was no point to the story, Yvan said abruptly, they didn't remain close. Christopher had dropped the friendship, as if his original pursuit had only been a cipher for another, more oblique kind of compulsion, although that had not prevented them from renewing their acquaintance when they ran into each other some years later.

That time, I had been there. It had been another chance encounter, not in the street this time but at a party, and had lasted only a few minutes before it was interrupted, the room was crowded with people. At the time Yvan had been just another one of Christopher's acquaintances, of which there were so many, but I remembered that I had liked him at once: his laconic manner, his slight air of indifference to the parade of his surroundings and still, and in particular, to Christopher's charm, to which so few seemed immune.

But as it turned out, Yvan was not a man of indifference—it was wariness, rather than indifference, that he felt toward Christopher, and not only because of their past. In some essential way Christopher was not a man to be trusted, and Yvan had intuited this. Once, I asked him when it had first occurred to him that we would end up together, in this arrangement—I made this odd choice of word, *arrangement,* as though it were a euphemism for something untoward— and he promptly replied, At once, from the very beginning, or at least so I wished.

Certainly, Yvan roused himself with surprising speed. I was still living in the apartment when we met and it was far too soon for a new relationship—Christopher had not moved out, he had merely made himself absent, the place was still filled with his things, intermingling with my things. The bedsheets had barely been changed. And although I was not very old, I was also not young. Moving onward so precipitously felt like the mark of a younger woman.

But Yvan asked me to move into his apartment right away, almost at the very outset of the relationship, so that the possibility of moving out of Christopher's apartment and into Yvan's presented itself as a very real scenario. It was undeniably convenient. And I was reminded of a biting and still unpleasant comment an acquaintance had once made over dinner: Women are like monkeys, they don't let go of one branch until they've got hold of another. This man—a friend of Christopher's first, but then also a friend of mine—had been seated beside me and across the table from his wife and Christopher.

When he spoke, he was looking at Christopher. He barely seemed aware of how clearly we—the women at the table, myself and his wife—could see his expression of frank contempt, or perhaps he didn't care, he was addressing himself to Christopher and not to either of us. From where I was sitting I saw him in profile, so that his sneer, the curl of his lip, was especially pronounced. Presumably he was not speaking of his own circumstances, or of his relationship with his wife, who sat quietly beside Christopher, minutely examining the tablecloth and the cutlery that sat upon it. ‒

But anything was possible. It was, for example, possible—that they had met under adverse circumstances, that she had been involved with another man and been reluctant to leave the shelter provided by this man until she had secured the patronage, the commitment, of her current spouse (it was true that for as long as we had known them she had not worked, she was always well dressed and groomed, the kind of woman who knew where to get your hair blow-dried and nails manicured, information that is sometimes meaningless, but that also sometimes tells the entire story).

It was not pleasant to imagine the relationship between our friends in these terms, and yet it was surprisingly easy, an involuntary movement on the part of the imagination, which has no sense of decorum. Perhaps, even after years of marriage, the memory of her caution was a cause of dispute— there are men and women who cannot forgive a slight, however long in the past—perhaps one of the terms of the contract that underlay their marriage was the understanding that the husband would make the wife pay for this insult, this hesitation, again and again, over the course of their life together.

Nonetheless, I was offended on her behalf. Whatever the circumstance, it seemed terrible to be married to a man who was capable of saying such things about women, and in her presence, before other people—or rather, before another woman, one suspects men say such things among themselves all the time. From that point onward, I avoided this man, making excuses whenever Christopher proposed some activity, dinner or a weekend away in the couple's company, until Christopher accepted that I no longer wished to be friends with them. At least that was how he understood it, and I did not disabuse him of the notion, it was true that although my dislike had its origin in the husband, it had spread to the wife, in the milder form of discomfort—with her, I could no longer be at ease.

Several years later, the phrase still rankled— *women are like monkeys, they don't let go of one branch until they've got hold of another*— and it returned to me again, as matters with Yvan progressed. I knew that at a certain point, it no longer sufficed to say that the situation was complicated, the phrase did not buy you any time (although it *was* complicated, I was married and not formally or even publicly separated, I was still living in the old apartment, Christopher having gone I did not know where, he was initially staying with friends, then at a spare apartment belonging to his mother, usually rented out but now conveniently empty, which he told her he was using as an office).

No, at a certain point, one had to move forward, either by untangling the situation or by learning to live with its complications, the latter being the more common solution—people's lives grew messier as they grew older, then simplified again when they became truly old. Men were better at this, they were able to propel themselves through life, often a man was barely divorced before he was married again, it was merely a question of expedience, which was not cause for shame. Matters were different for a woman—women were more self-censoring, they excelled at it, having been taught to be so over a lifetime—and yet the emotions I felt for Yvan, so different from the man I had been married to, the man I was still married to, stubbornly failed to dissipate.

I did move into Yvan's apartment, three months after Christopher and I separated. Yvan's work as a journalist provided him with a comfortable but not lavish lifestyle. He had far fewer things than Christopher, but those things seemed to matter more, to be more accommodating, and I placed my own belongings in among them with surprising ease. We lived in the apartment, often we would work in the same room together, eat our meals and get into bed without parting company. Although it was much smaller than Christopher's apartment, as a couple we seemed to require less; it was discord that had required all that space.

And soon enough, Yvan began encouraging me to finalize the separation from Christopher, or at the very least tell him that I was no longer living in the old apartment, at present Christopher did not even know this. At first Yvan was hesitant, he seemed uncertain as to what his rights were—the progress of a relationship, for good or bad, can always be described through the accumulation or the disbanding of rights—but as the affair continued, now that I was living in his home, he made it clear that I was putting him in an awkward position, he only wanted to know where he stood.

Which was a fair request, I knew that myself. From a merely logistical point of view, it was vital I tell Christopher that I had left the apartment. What if there was a leak, what about the mail that was accumulating in the post box? These were simple matters, practical ones. Why then did I hesitate to call Christopher and tell him what was unlikely to be a blow, was it because of the previous acquaintance between Christopher and Yvan? Or was it because Christopher had asked me not to tell anyone about the separation, a request to which I had agreed, despite the fact that I was already living in another man's house, a man who was in fact his friend?

For obvious reasons this indecision—what might become for Yvan and me, as with the couple we had dined with, a fatal hesitation—had to be kept from Yvan. I told him that I would tell Christopher—precisely what I would tell Christopher, we never specified. He never demanded that I ask Christopher for a divorce outright, perhaps he sensed that this would be going too far, and in any case, it was humiliating to force a woman to ask her husband for a divorce, a woman should offer such a thing of her own free will, in order to be with the man she loves.

But the longer I stayed in Gerolimenas and waited for Christopher, the more the desire to actually confront him seeped away. I did not doubt the depth of my feelings for Yvan, but the issue began to feel like a question of administration rather than passion, a difficult thing to admit to oneself, much less to an impatient lover. Perhaps it was a question of age: *You cannot say you did it out of love, since at your age romantic passions have grown weak, and the heart obeys reason.*

And yet reason dictated that I could not be married to one man and live with another, at least not for very long. *The heart obeys reason.* What would be irrational would be to remain in this state of indecision, neither in nor out of the marriage, neither with nor free of this man. The sooner I was able to deliver myself from this situation the better, I could not remain beholden to two separate and antagonistic sets of expectation, I reminded myself that there were reasons why I needed to find Christopher, for my sake if not his.

Why don't I come out and join you? Yvan asked again.

I don't think that's a good idea, I said.

I worried that he would hear the response as too aggressive, too hostile, I wasn't trying to negate his anxieties, although I didn't exactly want them to blossom either, that would do neither of us good. I continued, It would muddy the water, I don't want to involve you in this, that doesn't seem fair to anybody, and before I could go much further he cut me off, he said, Of course, you're right, it's only that I miss you. I miss you too, I said.

We talked a little longer, I told him about the hotel, about the girl Maria—he found the idea that Christopher might have seduced her immensely entertaining, that was, he said, exactly the kind of thing Christopher would do, he was thoroughly perverse, but in a way that was somehow—*chic,* he said, the inverted commas around the word were audible in his voice. We both laughed, it was a good moment, it was as though we were discussing a mutual friend, of whom we were both fond, and in some ways that was true.

I told him again, before we said good-bye, that there was no reason for him to worry, Christopher was unlikely to object to my request for a divorce, he had seemed indifferent the last time we spoke, mostly he had been in a hurry to get off the phone, as if he had somewhere he needed to be. It was the first time I had used the word *divorce,* and I felt rather than heard the explosion of Yvan's happiness. It's an awkward situation but nothing more, I continued, once Christopher returns I will tell him that I want a divorce and then it will be over, then it will be mostly a matter of paperwork. In that case, Yvan said, and I could hear that he struggled to keep his voice light, I hope he returns soon.

4.

Later that afternoon, I hired a taxi and drove to one of the small villages inland. I imagined Christopher must have done the same at some point—there was only so much time you could spend on the terrace, by the pool, or otherwise within the confines of the hotel before tedium set in.

I said to Kostas that I wanted to see the surrounding area. He tried to explain that there was nothing to see. I said this could not be the case, there were miles of country stretching behind us. Eventually, he reluctantly mentioned a nearby church with some frescoes that had been impressive once, until they had been defaced by members of the local Communist Party.

I said that sounded fine, it sounded interesting. He immediately backtracked, flipping through a pile of brochures and leaflets in search of some other option with which to tempt me. There were a number of excursions he could suggest, or he could reserve a table at a popular restaurant one village over along the shore. That village was larger than Gerolimenas, there were bars, even a nightclub. Or I could hire a boat, there was a nearby island with wonderful beaches that was well worth seeing, he could recommend it.

I told him I preferred to go to the church, perhaps I would try the restaurant and the island another day. He still seemed to hesitate, I told him that I only wanted to get a little air, a change of scene. It did not need to be anything spectacular. At last, he shrugged and called the local taxi company and ordered a car. As he hung up, he warned me again that it was not impressive, just a local church, very small and virtually defunct, it was not what people came to the area to see. They came for the sea, for the beach, for the view . . .

It began to rain as we drove out of the village. I asked the driver his name, he said it was Stefano. I asked him if he knew Kostas and Maria. Yes, he said, he had known them his entire life. They had grown up together. Maria in particular—she was like a sister to him. I said that it was a small village. He nodded. Everybody knew everybody, and nobody ever left. I asked if people moved to the cities, to Athens for example. He shook his head. There are no jobs in Athens, the unemploy-ment rate is the highest it has ever been.

Then we sat in silence. Outside, the entire landscape was black from the fires. We drove up through the hills, away from the shore. The vegetation had been decimated, replaced by mounds of burnt charcoal, a lunar landscape. Row after row of the curious forms stretched across the ground. In places there was smoke still rising up from the ground—the fires had been burning as little as a week ago, Stefano said, they had only recently succeeded in putting them out after weeks, after months of burning.

I asked Stefano how the fires had started and he said it was arson. I waited for him to continue. A feud between two farmers, apparently it was over stolen livestock. The livestock wandered all over the place, he said, who knew which animals belonged to whom? One goat ends up in the wrong field, it was hardly a matter that called for retribution. But of course the farmers did not think, they made crazy accusations, first one and then the other, each claim more outrageous. They began actually stealing animals from each other, from stolen livestock it was only a small step to vandalism, the situation escalated, more and more people became involved—family and friends, then extended family and friends of friends—and then suddenly the entire country-side was burning.

An absurdity, he said. It was hard not to agree, there was an unbridgeable gap between the fact of missing livestock, a goat, a cow, a sheep, and the devastation that surrounded us. It was not so simple, he explained, the matter was a modern-day blood feud, the livestock and the fires were simply the latest iteration of something that renewed itself every year. The way the earth does, he said, and will do again after the fires—with spring there will come a new feud, about something else but really it is the same thing, this is a country addicted to fighting.

Especially in Mani, he said the area was known for its fierce history of fighting, the Maniots—as the people of Mani were called—were known for being very independent but it was hard to know what that independence had been good for. There is nothing here, he said. Look, you can see—there is nothing but rocks, the place is a collection of rocks. We have fought for our independence and our land and all we have to show for it is a collection of rocks.

He turned the car down a narrow one-lane road, here the vegetation had not burnt to the ground but had somehow melted, along both sides of the road stood drooping cactuses, their arms folding forward and their edges singed. The smell was terrible. The land was rotting, Stefano said. It had smelled like this all summer. By the coast, where the hotel was, the smell dissipated, the wind carried it off to sea, but farther inland the stench had accumulated, day after day. It had been worst at the height of summer, when the temperatures had been very high and the smell so heavy you could barely breathe.

A small stone church was visible on the horizon. There was nothing in its vicinity, only the burnt landscape. We drove up to the church. There were crushed and rusted cans in the charred grass outside, all manner of debris. Graffiti had been scrawled across the stone exterior—large Greek characters that I struggled to decipher, *lambda*, *phi*, *epsilon*, I spoke and translated French. Further marks had been carved into the wooden doors, the place was in very bad condition, it did not seem as if anyone was responsible for its care, it was hard to imagine a congregation gathering there. Stefano turned the engine off and shrugged, his face clouded.

It's nothing much, it is nothing worth seeing.

Is it in use?

Oh yes, he said. He looked a little surprised. Of course.

I opened the car door. The drizzle of rain was instantly absorbed by the soil, which remained dry. Stefano asked if I needed an umbrella, he thought he might have one in the trunk. I told him I was fine, the rain itself was warm and not unpleasant. He shrugged and got out of the car. I followed him to the double doors of the church, which he pulled open, evidently nothing was locked around here. He stepped back and gestured toward the dim interior. He reached into his pocket and took out a packet of cigarettes, then said that he would wait outside.

I switched on the light—a single electric bulb came on with a loud buzz. It did very little to illuminate the interior. After a moment, my eyes adjusted to the darkness. It was true that it was a humble space, several rows of wooden benches, a simple altar and reliquary. The church was Byzantine, probably twelfth or thirteenth century, there was a large fresco on three of the walls. The faces on the fresco had been rubbed out and the effect was strange, a row of saints standing blind and faceless, rendered anonymous by a likewise unidentified hand.

More characters had been written across the wall inside in paint—they did not seem as if they had been written by the same person or persons who had defaced the exterior of the church, the paint was another color, more faded despite the evident lack of sunlight inside, the jumbled characters differently formed. From the entrance, Stefano smoked. I asked him what the graffiti said. Carefully, he ground out the cigarette before leaning over to retrieve the butt.

He entered the church, quickly making the sign of the cross before stopping in front of the fresco. This is from the civil war. He stepped forward and touched the wall. The Communists defaced the saints—literally defaced them, he said with a grim smile, you see—and wrote some stupid Communist propaganda. You can't see all the characters, some of it is covered, but it says, he translated, *United Front from Below.*

He pointed to a row of characters, large parts of which had been covered. I saw that it was not a single piece of graffiti as I had initially thought, but two separate messages written at two different times, the first set of characters imperfectly blacked out and only partially covered by the second set. Stefano moved his fingers and pointed to the second set of characters. The army came and covered the Communist slogan and wrote their own slogan, *Athens Is Greece*. But you can see they did a sloppy job of it. So parts of the original Communist slogan are still visible, *Uni*—and—*elow*, if you read the whole thing together, it is nonsense, a nonsense phrase, *Uni Athens Is Greece Elow*.

He continued. They thought it wasn't enough to paint over the old slogan with their own message, they also scratched their message into the stone, only they didn't finish the job. I peered at the stone surface, it was true, someone had scored a few characters in—they only measured a few inches in height, much smaller than the sprawling graffiti below, which had been painted with a freer hand, after all it was much more difficult to carve into stone—and then abruptly stopped, as if they had been interrupted or perhaps decided it wasn't worth the effort.

It is extraordinary, I said to Stefano, as a record of the conflict. He shrugged, the church is much older than this political argument, many centuries older, in another country it would have been cleaned up, there would have been money to preserve the church, to make repairs, but here?

I nodded. He waited a moment, as if to see whether or not I had any further questions. Then he turned and retreated outside. I stayed only a few minutes longer, I did not want to keep Stefano waiting—although I saw that he had already lit another cigarette, probably he would have been happy enough to wait, after all the meter was running on the fare. It was cool inside the church, a respite from the dry heat outside. I stood before the line of blank-faced saints, I had never seen anything like it. As we returned to the car I asked Stefano what else I should see, I had the rest of the afternoon and I wanted to tour the area.

You could go to Porto Sternes, it is not too far, a little way down the peninsula. There are some very nice ruins on the beach, of a church. They say that the entrance to Hades is located in a cave at Porto Sternes—the tourists like it, although it is nothing more than a cave, a very nice cave, a big one even, but still just a cave. I said in that case I thought I could do without, although I liked the association between myths and ordinary places, places you could go to, perhaps if my stay extended further I would go.

What has brought you to Mani? Stefano asked. It was a reasonable question to which I could not think of a response. For a holiday, in order to relax, I was taking a break, I've always wanted to come to Greece. When I didn't reply he continued, Most of the people who come to the village do not leave the hotel, maybe they go to the beach or to one of the islands. They are never interested in seeing the interior.

As he spoke, we were driving inland, through a village. There were small single-story houses on either side of the road. The houses were built from concrete rather than stone, entirely charmless, it was true there was nothing much to see. Dogs roamed the street and the front yards were cordoned off by wire fences. In places, lengths of wire had come undone from the stakes. Plastic chairs stood outside the houses, warped and yellowed by exposure to the sun. It had nothing in common with Gerolimenas, an essentially picturesque village. This, rather than Gerolimenas, was the place where Stefano, and Maria, and Kostas, were from.

The driver was still watching me in the rearview mirror, he repeated the question—What has brought you to Mani? I had a brief impulse to reply in earnest—there might be relief in articulating my situation to someone, the purpose behind my visit, its perplexing duration, which was still undecided. Why not this man, essentially a stranger, one not obviously sympathetic, but also not unsympathetic? He might, for example, have driven Christopher at some point, he might even know where he had gone. But I did not. I said instead, without entirely knowing why, not even where the words came from, I'm working on a book about mourning.

The words sounded false as soon as I spoke them, the thinnest of fictions. Had Stefano met Christopher at some point, he would have known the explanation to be untrue, it was highly unlikely that two tourists would be writing two separate books about mourning. But to my surprise and relief, the explanation did not seem especially implausible to Stefano, he appeared interested and even pleased. He said that was not the usual reason why people came to Mani but it was a good reason, an interesting reason that he could understand, much better than the tourists who came for the beaches.

Had I come for the weepers, he asked. And I replied, Yes, exactly. And then could not think of anything further to say. Luckily he continued, had I ever heard a weeper, it was an amazing thing, very beautiful, very moving. No, I said. I've never heard one, I've only heard recordings— this was untrue and I had no idea why I continued to elaborate the meaningless lie, I had to hope that he would not ask me to describe the recordings, or tell him where I had obtained them, perhaps weepers did not allow their grieving to be recorded and he had known at once that I was not telling the truth.

I would have liked to change the subject but he was too enthused, he said to me that in fact his great-aunt was a widely admired weeper, one of the very best in the region. Sometimes she traveled great distances in order to mourn, people hired her even when there was a local woman available. It was too bad there wasn't a funeral for me to attend, unfortunately nobody had died in any of the local villages. He said this without a trace of morbidity, he was only being practical. If I had come a month earlier! he said. Several people had died in the fires and the country had been full with the sound of weeping. His great-aunt and a friend of hers, who often sang together, had traveled from funeral to funeral, singing the entire way, they had poured their ululation—the music of grief—into the air.

I said that I was sorry to have missed it, an idiotic thing to say, but he did not seem to notice. It was a dying practice, he said abruptly. None of the younger generation wanted to become mourners, it was not even practiced in very many places outside of Mani. He thought this was a terrible shame. It was not that he was a traditionalist, he said. But nowadays, girls wanted to be famous, they wanted to be on television, they dressed like prostitutes and then were surprised when they were disrespected. He fell into a brooding silence, it was obvious he was talking about someone in particular.

At any rate, your friend Maria does not seem like that, I said, she seems like a very sensible girl. He was silent for a moment—his face had brightened at the thought of the woman and then darkened again, clearly there was some kind of impediment. Yes, he said at last. She is almost too sensible, she is a very practical girl. This is a great virtue but it also can make her a little hard. She does not appear to suffer fools easily, I said. He agreed. That is certainly true, she is sometimes impatient, it shows in her manner, she does not hide anything, she is incapable of being deceitful, and he sounded proud, almost as though he were bragging.

What does such a woman want, I asked, what does she hope for? (Was it in fact my husband?) What does she hope for? he repeated. To get married, to have children, to live in a nice house. His voice was irritated. This was impossible, no woman had so limited an imagination, Maria would be no exception. She had seemed to me ambitious, even if her ambitions did not necessarily mean that she wished to find herself gyrating on national television, even if her ambitions were for nothing more than escape, in some as yet undefined form.

I thought Stefano must know this, he looked ill even as he spoke. The proverbial heart, beating on his sleeve. I expected to feel pity—although I did not know what had taken place between Maria and Christopher, or what was transpiring between her and the driver—but instead I felt an affinity with this man, I had none of the clarifying distance of pity. This despite the fact that the reasons for this affinity—if indeed that was the word—were thin at best, there was nothing we shared other than the fact that we had both, hypothetically, been betrayed.

But only hypothetically, and only betrayal of a kind: we had no claims on these people, or merely partial and imperfect ones. Stefano had no formal claim but he had the weight of his affection; I had the legal claim but not the authority of love. Together, we might have had the right to be outraged or jealous, but as it was we had nothing but a private well of feeling. In my case, I thought, that feeling was increasingly ill-defined, as my life with Christopher began to recede into the past, everything that I learned about him—a meaningless detail from his new life, a revelation from his past one—was a source of potential discomfort, causing a pang of greater or lesser pain, or even occasional indifference. This was the process by which two lives were disentangled, eventually the dread and discomfort would fade and be replaced by unbroken indifference, I would see him in the street by chance, and it would be like seeing an old photograph of yourself: you recognize the image but are unable to remember quite what it was to be that person.

But Stefano—who knew whether his passion would also give in to this lassitude, or whether it would prove stronger and endure. Would he eventually marry another girl—there was another girl, whether or not he was aware of it, aware of her, he was a handsome man and for a handsome man there is always another girl—but still tend to the embers of his original love? People were capable of living their lives in a state of permanent disappointment, there were plenty of people who did not marry the person they hoped to marry, much less live the life they hoped to live, other people invented new dreams to replace the old ones, finding fresh reasons for discontent.

I watched Stefano as he chewed on his lip and stared at the road. He did not strike me as one of these inventors of discontent. He knew what he wanted, it was not even necessarily out of reach, although persuading the unwilling into love was a hazardous endeavor, and one that only rarely succeeded. Unfortunately, it is difficult to convince someone that they need something they cannot see the purpose of.

It began raining again as we reached the hotel. Stefano hesitated a moment before he switched the engine off, and then asked if I wanted to meet his great-aunt, the weeper. He was quick to add that I wouldn't be able to hear the actual weeping—She doesn't do it on order, he said, somewhat illogically, as I thought that was precisely what she did. But I would be able to talk to her, he said, to interview her, *interview her,* he repeated the phrase, as if it were foreign to his tongue.

I said that would be useful. I couldn't think of any other response that would sound logical, I was supposedly in Mani researching the region's mourning rituals, in my position Christopher would have accepted Stefano's offer without hesitation. Perhaps in fact he had—if the great-aunt was so renowned a mourner, wasn't it more than likely that Christopher had sought her out? He might even have shared with her his research and travel plans, the mystery of his current location. Stefano checked his watch, he said he thought his great-aunt would be home now, it was just after the time of her afternoon nap—she was old, she needed a siesta—if I was free, we could go and have a cup of coffee with her.

I said that sounded good. He took out his cell phone and dialed as I sat in the back of the car. He spoke only briefly before hanging up, his voice had been jovial, he was probably a good son to his mother, a man who cared about family. It's fine, he said, I told her you were my friend, she is very happy to meet with you. We can explain about the book later. He started the engine and added that it was not far, only ten miles inland. We drove back down the road we had just traversed, Stefano was talkative, he seemed pleased to be introducing his great-aunt to me, pleased that I was coming. There was something almost disingenuous to his manner, I wondered again if he had driven Christopher, perhaps even to his great-aunt's house, he might have spoken the same words, *She is very happy to meet with you, her house is not far.*

We soon approached another village, very similar to the one we had just driven through, a collection of low-slung houses along another single-lane road. He stopped the car in front of a small white house, there was laundry hanging from a line and plastic flowers in pots by the door, even from the outside it was somehow both threadbare and carefully tended. That impression did not change as we went up the front steps, Stefano knocking on the door before swinging it open—he now seemed younger, like a boy returning home at the end of the school day—and calling to his great-aunt, who appeared at once.

She greeted us with a smile, then shook her head apologetically as Stefano explained that she spoke no English. As she waved us into the kitchen and pulled out a chair for me she continued smiling, she seemed almost unremittingly cheerful. Nescafé? she asked—a question I could understand—and I nodded. Soon, the three of us were around a small table (it was covered in a vinyl tablecloth with a bright pattern of cherries and strawberries, garish but easy to clean) with cups of instant coffee, thin and bitter.

I asked her how long she had lived in the village, and after waiting for Stefano to translate, she replied, All my life, which Stefano translated back into English. I nodded, we continued in this way, each morsel of conversation passed back and forth by Stefano, the conversation unfolding more slowly than it otherwise might have. I was more often used to being in Stefano's position—one of transmission, but also one of understanding—however, I found that I did not mind, in a curious way it took the awkwardness out of the situation. It was not exactly like speaking to a stranger, not for either of us, since in a way she was speaking not to me but to Stefano, her eyes moving back and forth between the two of us.

As I looked at Stefano and his great-aunt, tracing out the unlikely family resemblances between them, a crease at the eyes, the angle of the jaw, I thought of Christopher. Of my husband, who might so easily have been here, only a few days earlier. I almost thought I felt his presence in the room with us, he might have sat in this exact seat, opposite these exact people, looked at them exactly as I now looked at them. But what he would have made of them I did not know, I could not guess the questions he might have asked. As always, I returned to the absence that was at the heart of my experience of him.

I almost asked the great-aunt then if she had

met Christopher, if he had been here in real life and not supposition. But I couldn't locate the words, I didn't know how I would phrase the question, and after a moment, I asked the great-aunt about the fires instead, whether she knew any of the parties involved. She laughed, her body shaking a little, she was short but not a small woman, her body looked as if it was made of compacted flesh, she was wearing a flower-print dress but her features were androgynous, perhaps by nature or perhaps by age. She knows every-one, Stefano said. The men behind the arson—she says they are boys. They are men, but they are boys. She smiled, nodding as he spoke, as if she understood English perfectly.

Should he ask about the weeping, Stefano said, lowering his voice and leaning toward me. I was startled, I had almost forgotten the reason for our visit, quickly I replied. How long have you been a weeper? It was an inane question, I felt immediately self-conscious, I almost thought Stefano gave me a look of reproach, perhaps the question was too blunt. Christopher would undoubtedly have made a better job of it. But Stefano promptly translated the question and the reply, My mother was a weeper, and so was my aunt, it is in the family, there was no question that I would not also become a weeper, once it became obvious that I could do it.

When did you realize you could?

When I was very young. Like I said, my mother and my aunt were both weepers, they would sing together, I remember being a child and hearing them perform at a funeral. I would sit with the bereaved, and I would watch them begin the wailing, they were famous, they performed together. So I was young when I began trying to sing. And I learned, they taught me first to sing, then to channel the sadness that is necessary to weeping.

They taught you this when you were only a child?

Even children have experience of sadness. At first, when I was a young woman, I would think about sad stories that I had heard, about soldiers who had been killed at war, and the wives and girlfriends who waited for them in vain. Eventually, as I became older, I had my own losses to call upon, and it became easier: I lost my father, my brother, then my husband, at this point in my life there is no shortage of inspiration.

So you think of a personal loss?

Yes. The songs themselves, they are fixed lamentations, they tell stories. But in order to really feel the songs, in order to trigger the emotion that you need to lament, I need to think about something personal, it is hard if it remains abstract. This is one reason why you become better as you grow older, when you are young, you do not have an intimate experience of death, of loss, you do not have enough sadness in you to mourn. You need to have a great deal of sadness inside you in order to mourn for other people, and not only yourself.

Her eyes were twinkling as she said this and she smiled, as if she had made a joke. Then she cleared her throat and looked at Stefano, as if waiting for him to ask the next question.

Do you think she would be willing to sing for me?

He seemed to hesitate—he had already told me it was unlikely—but then asked the question anyway. She paused, adjusting the folds of her skirt with her hands. She cleared her throat again and then began to sing. Her voice was low and throaty, she began almost tentatively, as if growing accustomed to its weight, raising one hand in the air as she sang in a series of atonal registers. She seemed then to find the thread she had been seeking, her fingers pulled together against her thumb as though she were drawing it through the air.

Her voice, as it unfolded across the room, was not beautiful. It was heavy, as heavy and awkward as the boulders that marked the Mani landscape, a collection of rocks. The notes dropped out of her mouth and tumbled across the room, first one and then the next and then the next. They accumulated, the room was soon full of their discordance. She continued, her voice growing in volume, the objects in the room vibrating, the sound of her singing transforming the kitchen interior where we sat. She began slapping her hand against the table, she closed her eyes and then she rocked back and forth, her hand still keeping rhythm.

Her voice raised an octave or two, she began to make a high keening sound, and as I listened, transfixed, I saw that there were tears gathering in her eyes, which she had opened very slightly, her head still tilted back. The tears rested on the bottom rim of her eye for a long moment before slowly trickling down. She paused for a ragged intake of breath and then continued, as if she were in a trance, her eyes now wide open, the lamentation pouring out of her, her face wet with tears.

I looked at Stefano, I wanted her to stop—she was in pain, and to what purpose? I felt at once the extent of my deception: I was not writing a book, I was not researching the ritual of mourning, there was nothing I could learn from her grief, whose authenticity I did not doubt. Notwithstanding the fact that it was a performance, essentially on demand, the entire situation a fabrication. And I understood that this was why she was paid, not because of her vocal capabilities, not even for the considerable strength of her emoting, but because she agreed to undergo suffering, in the place of others.

She did stop at last, and Stefano handed her a tissue, which she used to wipe away her tears. She took a glass of water, she did not make eye contact with me, I thought she looked—as she drank the water and waved away Stefano's concerned attentions—embarrassed, as though she had been caught making a scene. I too felt embarrassed and soon stood up. She waved good-bye in a halfhearted way. I didn't know how to ask Stefano about leaving some money for her so I left some bills on a table by the door. It didn't feel like the right thing to do, I saw Stefano glance at the bills, but he didn't say anything. It was still raining when we left, and we walked quickly to the car to avoid the rain.

In my room, I sat down on the bed. Despite the rain, the window was open and the fan overhead turned in slow, rhythmic circuits. I was exhausted, the afternoon had physically depleted me. I was not easy with the deception—the impersonation of Christopher, or at least his interest in Mani, his reason for being here, an act of duplicity that had taken me all the way into that house, that kitchen—still less with the phantom sense I'd had of my husband, sitting at that table, the odor of his presence even stronger than it had been in his abandoned room.

It had been three days since I had arrived, and there was still no sign of Christopher. For the first time, I felt a sense of panic—what if something had happened? I had to admit to myself that I was not clear about what my responsibilities were in this situation, Christopher had every right to disappear without being hounded by me. But hadn't he been gone too long without word, wasn't there something strange, something wrong about Christopher's absence? I called the front desk and asked for a list of hotels in the neighboring villages, without specifying why. The list was not long, within five minutes Kostas had called back with the telephone numbers.

I immediately telephoned all the hotels. He was not staying in any of them, or if he was he was not using his name—although why would he stay in a hotel under a false name, even the notion was ridiculous—and I hung up, uncertain. Perhaps I should have asked Stefano outright if he had driven Christopher, if he knew where he had been planning to do his research, perhaps he even knew the driver Christopher had ultimately hired, it wasn't impossible. A moment later, the telephone rang. It was Kostas, he asked if I needed anything further. I told him that I was fine. He hesitated, then said that Christopher had been seen yesterday in Cape Tenaro, not too far from Gerolimenas. I felt an immediate wave of relief, which was subsequently replaced by irritation—the entire time I had been waiting,

Christopher had merely been sightseeing—I asked Kostas if he knew when Christopher would be back.

He said no, nobody from the hotel had spoken to him. He paused and then said, A friend of Maria's saw him, he was with a woman. I was too surprised to respond. She is very upset, she is crying, he continued, and for a moment I didn't know who he was referring to. I'm sorry, I said. Who has been crying? Maria, he replied, she has been crying, it is a real nightmare. Oh, I said, and then added without knowing why, I'm sorry. Don't worry, Kostas replied, and he sounded cheerful, as if he were speaking of nothing of consequence, She'll be fine. But would you like to arrange a car, would you like to go to Cape Tenaro to join your husband?

No, I said. My face was hot and I no longer wished to be speaking on the phone, I had to keep myself from hanging up at once. Kostas was silent and then said, Of course, and that I should let him know if there was anything further he could do. I told him that I would stay another night but no longer, that I was looking for a flight that would return to London the next day. Very good, he said. I hope you've enjoyed your stay with us. Yes, I said. Thank you, I have. I hung up and then I called Yvan and told him that I was coming home, and he said good, without asking any questions he said, Good, I am glad.

5.

I walked down to the sea, I did not want to remain in the hotel any longer. I left my things on the beach—it was a harsh and rocky shore, hardly luxurious, the landscape something more than picturesque, edging toward a bleak and extreme blankness—and swam out into the water. It was cold but the water was calm and I went far, well past the buoys and the edge of the cliff, to where the bay opened up into ocean.

I was an infrequent but relatively strong swimmer. The cold was bracing, exactly what I needed: it was impossible to think in the face of it. When I was tired I stopped and rested, treading water before resuming, over time my breath grew short and I did not recover so easily, then I floated on my back and stared at the sky—the color white rather than blue, so that the face of the cliff graded imperceptibly into the atmosphere—and then, as I flipped myself upright, down to the black and blue of the water. I closed my eyes against the sun's glare and then reluctantly turned and began swimming back to shore. I had gone farther than I intended, I did not know how long I had been in the water.

There were several things I would need to do in order to organize my departure, deferred more than once and now suddenly imminent—the ticket, the packing, the phone call to Isabella. This time, I hardly stopped to rest and by the time my feet touched the bottom—the surface rocky, so that I winced in pain and lifted them at once—I was exhausted and gasping for breath.

When I stepped out onto the shore, two men shouted to me from the embankment, a young woman translated: They say it's too cold, it's too late in the season for swimming. I said that I was fine and they shook their heads, they had been watching, they half expected to call a rescue boat but I was a strong swimmer, I had returned to shore without problem, they were impressed. They saw that I had only stopped twice for breath, barely at all, that was very good, better me than them. I shouted my thanks and they waved before resuming their own conversation.

This meaningless interaction raised my spirits, it was the first time I had spoken to anyone in Gerolimenas apart from the staff at the hotel, they had been friendlier than I expected. As I walked back to the hotel, I remembered Stefano's disdain for the tourists who flocked to the area, it was not difficult to imagine what the villagers must think of me, I was exactly the kind of person they would despise. An outsider, rich—at least relatively speaking, I was staying at the big hotel rather than the more humble establishment at the opposite end of the village's main road, which hardly seemed to attract any foreigners—a city dweller, a tourist.

A tourist—almost by definition a person immersed in prejudice, whose interest was circumscribed, who admired the *weathered* faces and *rustic* manners of the local inhabitants, a perspective entirely contemptible but nonetheless difficult to avoid. I would have irritated myself in their position. By my presence alone, I reduced their home to a backdrop for my leisure, it became *picturesque, quaint, charming,* words on the back of a postcard or a brochure. Perhaps, as a tourist, I even congratulated myself on my taste, my ability to perceive this charm, certainly Christopher would have done so, it was not Monaco, it was not Saint-Tropez, this delightful rural village was something more sophisticated, something unexpected.

Christopher on the loose in this place—I laughed, I could not help it, it was a terrible thing to imagine. The combination of his charm and erratic sympathy, his persistent inability to imagine the reality of other people's situations—it was no wonder he was causing such havoc. Suddenly, I was glad I had come to Mani in order to ask for a divorce. I imagined journeying this far in hopes of a reconciliation, only to find Christopher roaming the countryside, chasing one woman after another. Briefly my eyes were wet with tears.

I had reached the hotel, and went up the stone steps leading from the embankment onto the terrace. I thought with some relief that I had only one more dinner to eat at the restaurant, now that I had decided to leave, I could not wait, it could not happen soon enough. As I reached the lobby, I saw Maria and Stefano standing together by the desk. I realized it was the first time I had seen the pair together, despite the fact that they were stubbornly coupled in my mind. They appeared to be in the midst of conversation, perhaps even arguing.

Maria was dressed in her own clothes, she was wearing a pair of blue jeans and a blouse, I had never seen her wearing anything other than the hotel uniform and the effect was jarring. Both she and Stefano were almost unrecognizable; although they looked exactly as they always did, their demeanor, even from a distance, was entirely different from the manner they exhibited while they were working, it was enough to transform them into strangers. In their professional contexts they were polite, reserved to the point of being stilted, all the time they were conscious of being observed.

Here too, they were being observed—Kostas stood behind the desk, he was writing in a ledger, from time to time he lifted his head to look at them with a wry expression, once he even shook his head, it was obvious that this was not the first time he had seen the pair together, behaving in this manner—after all, they were standing in the middle of Maria's workplace, in the lobby of the hotel. And yet they seemed unconstrained by the setting, they were speaking loudly, gesturing with their hands and even shouting on occasion.

I stood by the entrance. Kostas watching Maria and Stefano, Maria and Stefano watching each other, their attention describing an almost geometric form. I had a towel around my waist, my hair and bathing suit were still wet—the sun had not been sufficiently strong or the walk long enough to dry them out, at least my sandals no longer left wet tread marks on the tiles—and I felt self-conscious opening the door and entering the lobby, it felt intrusive, ridiculous and somehow undignified. I sat down on one of the terrace chairs, perhaps they would leave before too long.

I continued to watch them from where I sat, the driver and the receptionist. Although at that moment there was not exactly an excess of affection between them, they were by no means an illogical couple, they looked well together, they made a handsome pair. They both had youth on their side, which was no small thing. In fact, Stefano was nicer-looking than Christopher, whose looks had long begun to dissipate from age. Seen like that, it was not difficult to imagine them in a passionate embrace, the dispute—assuming it was a dispute, but I did not see how it could be anything else, the signs were unmistakable—could simply be read as a lover's quarrel.

And yet it was not. I soon saw there was something in the nature of the exchange, the intimacy between them was not unqualified, they did not behave exactly like people who were sleeping together, not even like people who had slept together at some point in the past, or people who necessarily intended to in the future. I couldn't hear what they were saying from where I sat, of course they would not be speaking English. The glass doors reflected not only my own image but that of the water and the sky behind me, the jumble of chairs and tables on the terrace, the effect obscured the scene inside.

It was frustrating in the way that watching a film without the soundtrack can be, the mouths of the actors opening and closing but no words coming out. I wanted to hear their words, even though I knew I would not be able to understand what they were saying, and the entire affair was of course none of my business. I stood up and wrenched the door open and entered the lobby, sitting down on one of the chairs that was arranged near the desk. I worried that it was eccentric, sitting down in the middle of the lobby in my towel and bathing suit, I expected Maria and Stefano to turn and look at me, I expected Kostas to ask how he could help, if I needed anything.

But none of them reacted, it was almost as if I wasn't there. I sat in the chair and was transfixed despite myself, it was all too plausible that the problems of these particular people were related to my own—for example, I could not help but believe that the root of their disagreement was Christopher, it was a reasonable assumption. Kostas had said that Maria had been upset to hear about this other woman, that she had been in tears.

Maria said something in a loud, rough voice— as expected, they were speaking Greek, and in deciphering the substance of their conversation, I could only go by the tone and gestures they employed. However, I could observe all these more clearly, now that I was inside. As Maria spoke, she shook her head. She lifted her chin sharply and looked directly into Stefano's eyes as if she were issuing a challenge. I leaned forward, the damp from my bathing suit was soaking into the cushion, I worried it might leave a stain. Did water leave stains? Maria and Stefano continued to take no notice of me, for a moment I regretted not choosing a chair that was closer to the pair.

Now Stefano was speaking in a low and urgent tone. Maria was listening in sullen silence, eyes averted, he should have known better than to lecture her in that way, I couldn't understand what he was saying, but I recognized the hectoring tone all too well, he was patronizing her without being aware of it. Although Maria listened without interrupting, her expression remained sullen, she twisted her mouth into a grimace and continued to look away from him.

Whatever he was saying, it did not please her. Her face contorted, moving from one grimace to the next, passing through an extraordinary range of expressions, all of them unhappy. She no longer seemed attractive, her eyes were red and the lids were swollen from crying, it further weighted her already heavy features. I couldn't tell if Stefano noticed, it seemed to be the furthest thing from his mind, perhaps he was incapable of perceiving the alteration. He was gazing at her with adoration, although he was trying to be stern—or, at least, so I gathered.

Stefano continued speaking, as if he were afraid that if he stopped even for a moment, he would lose her conclusively. Now and again he gestured with his hands for emphasis, he leaned toward her imploringly. She did not reply. Even if he succeeded in persuading her—I speculated on what the finer points of his argument might be, it might have to do with Christopher (he was a waste of time, a treacherous and useless sort, I could not disagree) or it might have to do with something else entirely, it hardly mattered, I was certain that the real goal of all his discourse was to persuade her that she should love him, as he loved her—he would not win her, not in this way.

As if he sensed this, Stefano drew back,

exasperated, his face clouded, he made a small but distinct and even violent gesture of anger. That anger was not necessarily directed at Maria, but it was anger nonetheless, directed perhaps at Christopher, perhaps at the situation or himself. From his perch behind the desk, Kostas raised his eyes to look at me. I met his gaze for a moment, then looked away.

Maria let out a sudden and wordless cry. Both Kostas—who had been looking at me—and I turned to look at her. She was standing with her arms rigid and her eyes pinned to Stefano's face. Her own face, which was ashen, blank and inexpressive, was alarming. It was generally too expressive, it expressed things even when she did not mean to, even when there were not actually things to express. Now, although it retained its rounded fullness, it was as if it had been drained, the features had caved in. Stefano had turned away, he was still saying something, muttering to himself, but he would not look at her, he took a step toward the doors and then stopped, it was not so easy for him to leave her.

Maria then spoke, the words sounded harsh and rasping as she pronounced them. Behind his desk, Kostas let out a long and low whistle. Stefano's face—he was still standing with his back to Maria—slowly turned a deep and troubled red. He raised his hand, as if to strike the face of someone standing before him, but of course there was no one there, he had turned away from Maria—and it was Maria, this time, who was without doubt the object of his anger. He was shaking, his face was growing mottled, as if he were having difficulty breathing.

She had humiliated him in some way, and I knew then that he was aware that I sat in the lobby behind him, although he gave no new indication of seeing me, it was obvious. And I also knew that Maria was similarly aware of my presence, of the fact that I was watching them, and that she had used this in order to humiliate him further. My skin prickled, I felt newly uneasy. The chair was now soaking wet, when I stood up there would be a large stain. Kostas continued to observe them from behind the desk, as though he were providing color commentary at a sporting event, with an expression at once jovial and concerned.

Soon, Stefano appeared to regain control of himself, at least to some degree: he lowered his hand. But his face was still flushed, he had not entirely mastered his emotions, his physiognomy was giving him away. He was obviously a man who was capable of violence, like so many. I turned to look at Maria, I expected that she might show some sign of fear, it was not a pleasant sight—this man, with his strangulated emotions, his barely suppressed rage, it would not have been made better by the fact that she did not love him, that she already held him in contempt—but she was in no way cowed, she only stood with her hands pressed to her sides.

Then, she repeated the phrase—or I thought she did, the words sounded much the same as before, but the intonation was entirely different, if her expression had not been so stony, her posture so rigid, I would have sworn she was beseeching him in some way. And indeed, Stefano's posture seemed to soften, he turned his head a little, as if reconsidering. Yes—he was beginning to turn around, his face was hopeful, he was truly her slave, I had never seen a man so enthralled by a woman, and with so little effort on her part.

As she observed him, she briefly frowned, it was one of the quandaries a woman sometimes faces, not just a woman, but all of us: she entrances one man without effort, a man who is undesired, who follows her around like a dog, however much he is whipped or abused, while all her efforts to attract and then ensnare another man, the truly desired man, come to naught. Charm is not universal, desire is too often unreciprocated, it gathers and pools in the wrong places, slowly becoming toxic.

Her grimace was growing more and more self-reflexive, a smirk that was directed no longer at Stefano but at herself, she was obviously not unaware of the ironies of the situation. I did not see that either the situation or their respective positions had changed, her expression was not one that gave much hope. Nevertheless, Stefano reached forward and embraced her, using both arms to pull her body toward him. And although she did not appear to soften her posture, she also did not pull away. The result was an embrace that could not have satisfied Stefano, it was not unfriendly but it was certainly not sexual or romantic, she was only suffering his touch.

Still, it was clear to me that although she did not love him, she did not want to let him go. She wanted to keep it—whatever was taking place between the two of them—in play, in her back pocket, every woman needed a backup, at least every sensible one did. She was no fool, as Stefano had said, she was a practical woman, and although she stood stiff as a corpse in Stefano's arms, she did not repulse him in any definitive way, it was all open to interpretation. As she stood there, she might even have been contemplating a future with this man. On the one hand there was security and love, the possibility of children, on the other the well of his desire, which would have to be satisfied. The situation would only grow more suffocating with time—time, an entire life of it, of avoiding or scorning his touch. No doubt he would make her pay for her disdain, for the men she would have preferred to love.

The contempt she felt for the man who held her in his arms! And yet there were plenty of women who would have been only too delighted to love the driver, he was handsome and not without charm, and evidently he was capable of loyalty. There was of course the problem of his temper, but women could be surprisingly accommodating, as well as optimistic, one could live in the hope that his anger would subside, especially once he was loved in return, it was not impossible. Yes, it would have been better if she let him go—if she told him that she would never love him, that they had no future together.

But I saw, it was clear, that she had no intention of doing so. As I watched, she slowly raised one arm and stroked his back, a caress of sorts. The gesture was a lie, totally insincere, I could see her face from where I sat, the disjunction between its rigid expression and the gentle, intimate motion of her fingers was disturbing, her hand seemed to have a life of its own, like something from a horror movie. But Stefano, who could not see what I could see, took the gesture at face value, its effect was instantaneous. His features illuminated with such hope. He reached a hand up to stroke her hair and then hesitated, he didn't want to push his luck. She pulled away immediately, that was enough of that, her manner seemed to say.

Of course, Stefano was disappointed but he remained pleased, the situation was better than he thought, it was not, as far as he was concerned, entirely a lost cause. Maria still appeared disgruntled but at least she was not crying, or shouting, or even glaring at him, she merely looked as if she wished to dismiss him, she had things to do, she had wasted enough time talking with him in this way. In an instant, she had transformed herself into a professional woman, a busy one, she even looked down at her watch and frowned, she had lost track of the time, it was far later than she'd thought.

She said something to Stefano—abruptly, a terse good-bye, perhaps—he nodded and stepped back. She opened the door to the staff room, it was probably the start of her shift, she would need to change into her uniform, brush her hair, collect her thoughts. But then she turned and looked, not at Stefano, but at me. Her gaze was direct and unequivocal, it had an uncanny effect—as if an actor you have been watching on television suddenly turned to acknowledge you, the spectator. I was disconcerted, she nodded coldly, perhaps it was a necessary acknowledgment— we both knew that she knew that I had witnessed the scene. I admired the gesture, it was more than I would have done in her position, undoubtedly she was formidable in her way.

The door closed behind her. I looked to see where Stefano had gone, to my surprise I saw that he was now walking toward me. Abruptly, I took out my phone and peered down at it—as if I had been in the midst of writing an e-mail or reading my messages, the pretense was stupid and futile, it would have fooled no one. But I didn't know what else to do as I sat in the chair, waiting for him to approach, which he did with surprising rapidity. Within moments he was standing before me, his expression was friendly, a little sheepish, entirely unprepossessing.

His voice, when he spoke, was uncertain, he bore no similarity to the raging male, the passionate lover, I had seen only moments earlier. He spoke in English and while his control of the language was excellent, he naturally lacked the fluency he possessed in Greek. Listening to him, I realized that one of the reasons why he had seemed more appealing, more masculine, even when unsuccessfully wooing Maria, was his linguistic control. Even in that most undermining of situations, fluency had allowed him to be more assertive than he was in situations that called for English.

I came here looking for you, he said.

I looked at him with surprise, I had been listening to how rather than what he was saying, nonetheless the content of his words, the direct address of this statement, spoken in a flat and matter-of-fact tone, was impossible to ignore. It was obviously untrue, he had come to the hotel looking for Maria, in order to comfort her (she had been upset to learn that Christopher had been seen with another woman), or confront her (why must she be so upset?). I continued to look up at him blankly, without replying, I could not imagine what he could have to say to me, or the purpose of this lie.

Would you like to have dinner with my great-aunt this evening? he asked.

I hesitated, I did not understand, why would his aunt wish to see me again? When I did not respond, Stefano continued.

I can drive you.

He sounded hopeful. The invitation seemed genuine, it might have been a simple instinct for hospitality—I wondered if perhaps, after our day together, I was no longer simply a customer, my interest (borrowed from Christopher) in the traditions of the area having somehow stood me in good stead. It was as though he now felt an obligation to aid me in my mission, however poorly conceived and articulated, if he scratched only a little further, the pretense would collapse, I knew nothing about the subject.

I confess I felt a small wrench—I would need to decline, tell him it was impossible, that I was about to go upstairs and book my return flight to London, I had just been looking at flights on my phone. I had no reason to feel guilty but on the whole I was not good at disappointing people, even and especially people I did not know. I tried to avoid this type of interaction but generally only succeeded in postponing what was, from the start, clearly inevitable—wasn't that why I was here in Gerolimenas in the first place? No, when you were going to let people down it was better to do it as quickly as possible.

The only problem, I said, is that I am leaving, immediately. There has been a change of plan, I no longer need to stay.

You are not going to wait for your husband to return?

As far as I could recall, I had not told Stefano that I was married, much less that I was here waiting for my husband—it was not necessarily so startling, presumably everyone in the hotel knew (Maria would have told them, and if not Maria then Kostas). But he looked suddenly embarrassed, as if the words had slipped out by accident, he knew that he had broken a code, the tacit understanding that underscores our social interactions, whereby we pretend we do not know what we in fact do know.

This had been exacerbated by the times we lived in, I thought as I observed his deepening color, the age of Google searches and social media profiles, how much of our behavior is regulated by disavowed knowledge? But the Internet is not even necessary, sexual conduct or misconduct is often enough, a friend once told me the story of a date she had with a man she was interested in, he was a musician, she said up front that she found him sexually very attractive.

They had arranged to meet for dinner at a local restaurant that she didn't know. They both lived in a fashionable part of West London that was minutely documented in magazines, newspaper supplements and blogs, it was no small feat to suggest a restaurant that was unfamiliar to her. She agonized over what to wear, the usual conundrum of selecting an outfit for a first date— a question of making oneself desirable, but also a question of how much effort one chooses to reveal—was amplified by the fact that she was not familiar with the venue, was it casual or was it more formal, the kind of place where men were expected to wear a jacket?

Eventually she resorted to looking it up on the Internet. There, she learned that the restaurant was *a favorite of locals in this fashionable neighborhood* with a *spectacular menu* and a *cozy, romantic vibe*. This only served to heighten her anxiety—how was it that she didn't know this restaurant? What did it mean that she didn't know it and he did? Probably nothing, that was what she said when she called me, nervously, to describe what she was wearing, her green dress and black ankle boots.

I couldn't immediately recall either item and told her that she should send me a photo, which she did, taken in the full-length mirror of her bathroom, one hand on her waist in a semi-seductive pose, however she had cropped the photo at the neck, or rather the bottom of her chin, so that her face was not visible. I wasn't sure why she had taken the photo like that, the effect was a little eerie but the outfit was a good one, and I texted back my approval. Have fun, I think I added, although I should have known, when she sent me the self-decapitated photograph, that things were not likely to turn out well.

The restaurant was small, with perhaps only ten tables. When she arrived she saw that it was in many ways ideal for a first date, with dark-painted walls and candles and sprigs of wild-flowers on the tables, the daily menu was written in chalk on a board, not fashionable or flashy. She couldn't believe that she had never been there before, at the very least, she thought, she would know about a new restaurant, even if nothing came of the date itself.

As it turned out, the date did go well. It went so well that as they left the restaurant they decided to take a walk, it was an unseasonably warm night. They drifted without purpose, it was still light outside, they both lived in the neighbor-hood. But as they continued to wander, up the Portobello Road and all the way to Golborne Road, she began to grow nervous again, it was getting late, it had grown dark and although he had taken her by the arm when guiding her across the street, there had been scant physical contact, perhaps he was not so interested after all.

She was on the verge of despair when he came to an abrupt stop and said, indicating the small terraced house before which they were standing, This is me. She stopped, almost too nervous to speak. He continued, Would you like to come in for a coffee? She immediately wondered why he didn't ask her in for a drink instead, it was past eleven, a coffee was strange and even a little ambiguous but a drink is obvious, everyone knows what a man or a woman means when he or she says, Would you like to come in for a drink?

However, when she did not reply, he smiled and repeated the question, Would you like to come in for a coffee? This time, he leaned toward her as he spoke and smiled—she thought teasingly, so that she felt there was no longer any ambiguity, a coffee or a drink, what's the difference, and she blurted out, I can't, I have my period.

She was astounded to hear the words leave her mouth, she remembered that she had thought to herself, before she left her apartment, that although it wasn't ideal at least it meant that she wouldn't leap into bed with the man at once, thereby ruining everything. But now he stepped back, with an expression somewhere between amusement and disgust, as if to say, But I only asked if you wanted a cup of coffee, I didn't inquire after the status of your uterus, the availability of your vaginal passage. In reality, he

111

only said three words, Good night, then, before politely kissing her on both cheeks—she leaned, numb, into this formal and distant embrace—and disappearing into his terraced house, the door clicking shut behind him.

She was not surprised when he did not call. Her main regret, she said as she recounted the story to me, was that she could never go back to that wonderful restaurant, a mere ten-minute walk from her apartment. But what about the man himself, the attractive musician? Couldn't she call him, make a joke of it—after all, they had been getting along well, he had asked her into his house, they liked each other. All she had done was refer directly to what they both knew had been on the table, what else does such an invitation imply, at such an hour, but eventual coitus? She shook her head vehemently, no, never. Even the thought was enough to make her feel sick. And besides, she added, I no longer desire him. The whole thing is impossible.

Stefano was still standing before me. Having ruptured the pretense that he didn't know what I knew he knew, he nonetheless recovered quickly. His manner—which now seemed to say, Let us bring an end to these fabrications, I know that you know that I know, or something along those lines—made it difficult for me to take up or even respond to this transgression. I realized, belatedly, that Stefano must have known all along that my purported research was nothing of the kind, the flimsiest of excuses, he must have known from the beginning that I had come to Mani in search of Christopher.

Perhaps he had driven Christopher and guessed at our affiliation the moment I stepped into the back of his car. Or perhaps Maria had told Stefano, although Maria did not know everything about Christopher, she did not know, for example, that the absent husband was soon to be an ex-husband. Would she have been relieved, had she known it? Would she have been made hopeful, to learn that I had come to Gerolimenas to ask for a divorce, that I was cutting this man, essentially a philanderer, free? Would that have led her to imagine a future, marriage, a life together, with Christopher? Imagination, after all, costs nothing, it's the living that is the harder part.

I saw that Stefano was perturbed, no longer by his slip of the tongue, but by the announcement of my departure, which was, after all, what had caused his small indiscretion, it was the true matter at stake here. It seemed to cause him dismay, perhaps the fact of my existence—a wife was no small thing and I was not even in the abstract, I was a material presence in the hotel, I had barely left these three days, my being there must have been a source of constant consternation to Maria—had made his argument more persuasive, after all, it was absurd to be hankering after a man who not only had abandoned you but was, by all appearances, being pursued by his wife.

Would she grow more hopeful, would my departure be interpreted by Maria as some ceding of ground? Although it might not be in the end to her, it might easily be to the woman in Cape Tenaro, or the next woman, there would always be a next, particularly with a man like Christopher. Was that why Stefano was so eager for me to stay? This was assuming that Christopher was at the root of their disagreement. Stefano continued, But you should not leave, there is still a great deal to see in the area, I could show you, there are many attractions that can be easily reached, now is a good time, during the low season, there are not so many tourists.

Now I felt a wave of pity—he was so desperate, he appeared to know that his powers of persuasion were, in this situation, even more limited than they had been in his argument with Maria, there was something absurd about his attempt to convince me, virtually a stranger, to prolong my stay, he knew it himself, he was aware that his words had no purchase. He came to a stop, and then stood in silence before me.

I'm sorry, I said, and my voice was more brusque than I would have liked, but there's nothing to be done, I need to go back to London. I wish I could stay, I added, as if this might soften the blow, but he was already retreating, he had turned and walked away, out the front doors of the hotel, without stopping to say good-bye. I was baffled. I looked up and saw that Kostas was—of course—watching, that he had observed the entire exchange. He shrugged, Ignore him, he called out across the lobby, he is not having a good day.

6.

That evening, on what was to be my final night in Gerolimenas, I had dinner with Maria. It happened very naturally, although it was hard to hink of a situation more awkward—the wife and the mistress, sitting across the table from each other, making conversation. The awkwardness was compounded by the fact that she was still working, she wore her uniform and said before she sat down that her shift would not end for another thirty minutes, and that staff were not to fraternize with guests, not under any circumstances.

Her words had the quality of a formal announcement and for a moment she merely stood before me. It had not turned out well, the last time she had consorted with a guest of the hotel—neither of us said this but it was as if we both had the thought at the same time, her forehead creased and she stood immobile, staring down at the table, one hand on the back of the chair. She had asked if she could join me, but she now looked as if she might change her mind. She didn't, and at last she pulled the chair out and sat down.

I waited for her to say something. She must have had something to say—why else would she have asked to sit down, her manner when she did so was deliberate, as if she had been considering the action for some time, for some hours if not days, perhaps she was going to reprimand me for having eavesdropped on her conversation with Stefano—but she simply sat on the edge of her seat and looked around, she seemed anxious, perhaps she was worried that Kostas or someone else would appear and ask her what on earth she was doing. The waiters seemed not to notice her arrival, as if the sight of an employee sitting down to dinner with a guest was too bizarre to acknowledge.

I asked if she would like a glass of wine. She looked as if she were going to refuse, then shrugged and nodded. A glass of wine would be nice. I motioned to the waiter, who came to the table at once. He stood before me without looking at Maria, although they were colleagues and must have known each other.

I ordered a second glass of wine and then asked Maria if she had eaten dinner, I assumed she had not, it had been one in the afternoon when I had seen her in the lobby with Stefano and it was now past eight. She shook her head and I asked the waiter if he could bring another table setting, which he did, although he did not bring a second menu. Patiently, I asked him to bring a second menu but Maria said it wasn't necessary, she knew what she wanted.

She proceeded to order at length, in Greek, she was obviously familiar with the menu. The waiter, as she gave her order, listened impassively with his hands folded before him. He made none of the small movements and gestures waiters make to show their continued attention—the carefully inclined head, the murmured *very good* or *excellent choice,* the small nods here and there, all of which he had employed extensively when serving me before.

Nor did he write down her order. Instead he simply stared at her, hands folded in front of him, evidently affronted by her assurance. Even with my limited comprehension, I could tell that she was speaking to him as if he were there to serve her, not as if he were a colleague who happened to be temporarily placed in the role of server. He said nothing, even when she fell silent, and she said something sharply, still in Greek. He turned to me without saying anything in reply and asked in English if I had decided what I would like.

I ordered salad and a pasta, it was not the most inspiring choice, the pasta was nothing wonderful but I was tired of grilled meats and cheeses, the heavy Greek food—even the relatively cosmopolitan version that was served in the hotel restaurant—was not to my liking. The waiter nodded and said he would be back with the wine. He smiled as he took the menu and then left without looking at Maria, his rudeness was so pointed that I wondered if there was anything in it, some history of animosity between the two of them, he had seemed until then a thoroughly inoffensive man.

After the waiter left we fell silent, there was now nothing obvious to say, the business of ordering our meal having been got out of the way. I made several attempts at conversation, admittedly they were banal topics. But Maria appeared to have no intention of launching into the heart of the matter, the reason why she had asked to sit down, perhaps it had been a mistake to invite her to dine with me—perhaps she did not have enough conversation to fill the length of the meal and intended to sit in stony silence until the final course, whereupon she would finally unburden herself and say what she had sat down to say.

The waiter brought the wine. After another extended silence, I decided to broach the matter, I was now feeling certain that she had sat down not because of the earlier incident, but because she had something to tell me about Christopher— perhaps she needed money, perhaps she was pregnant, perhaps she wanted me to relinquish my rights to the man, she would tell me that they were in love and I was the only impediment, the thought passed through my mind—in which case I would tell her that I was neither liable nor an interested party, that I would be asking Christopher for a divorce, as soon as possible, as soon as he returned.

I asked Maria how long she had known Christopher, how it had come about, the phrasing was a little callous, I didn't like referring to whatever had happened as *it,* but didn't know what other word to use. I didn't know if it was as formal as an affair (that seemed unlikely given the relative brevity of Christopher's stay, it had been, I thought, less than a month), I didn't even know if anything concrete had taken place—by which I mean anything material, anything physical, it might have been only hope and innuendo.

But she immediately bristled, she looked at me as if I were pointlessly mocking her and I suppose it might have felt that way to her. After all, I was the wife, I appeared to hold all or at least many of the cards in this situation, despite the fact that I couldn't currently locate my husband, having traveled to this remote locale in the hopes of finding him. However much he might have betrayed me (and going by appearances and the information that she had, I would have been in a very desolate position indeed), no matter how threadbare the reality it represented, that title and position still had its symbolic power.

I thought she might not respond, and was about to signal to the waiter and order another glass of wine, it seemed like it was going to be a very long meal. But then she relented, as if remembering that she had been the one to create the situation by asking to sit down at my table in the first place, and she muttered something about having met Christopher on his very first day, upon his arrival. She was speaking in a low and virtually inaudible tone, I would need to ask her to raise her voice, a request that could be taken badly, luckily she seemed to be aware that I hadn't been able to hear her. She raised her eyes to meet my gaze and repeated, I met him the day he arrived, I was working at the front desk.

She said it as if she thought the timing gave her some greater claim to him, three weeks or thereabouts, the entirety of Christopher's stay in Mani. Compared to whoever it was he had been seen with in Cape Tenaro, it was virtually an eternity. Sitting across the table from her, I wanted to tell her that nonetheless, it was nothing compared to five years of marriage and three years of courtship before that, which again was nothing compared to a decade, two decades, the lifetime that could be spent in the company of one other person.

Now and again, over the course of our marriage, Christopher and I had seen or even spent time with elderly couples in their seventies or eighties, couples who had passed the entirety of their adult life together, and we had idly wondered if our own marriage would endure so long. Of late, we had known this was not going to happen. More to the point, we had known that even if we were each to fall in love again, it was unlikely that we would reach a fiftieth wedding anniversary with this new person, our probable life spans were against it, we had already failed in that respect.

For a moment, as I sat across the table from this strange woman, that mutual failure was like a bond that remained between Christopher and me, despite his absence and the vast distance between us, in the end we had experienced our mortality together. Perhaps because I did not respond, Maria continued, He was very friendly, very kind, most guests at the hotel treat the staff like trash or even worse, like nothing—as though you don't exist, as though you are thin as air. He arrived alone, she added defensively, although I had not said anything, he arrived alone and when I asked how many guests were staying, he made a point of saying that it was only him, that he was by himself.

Of course, he would have. But on the other hand, what was to say that this was not a matter of interpretation? Perhaps he had merely been making conversation, or perhaps he was even being practical (if he was alone, he would only require one key, one place setting at breakfast, for example). But it seemed cruel to point this out and I could see the scene clearly enough, Christopher had always known how to make an entrance, it was his departures that needed work. I wondered how long it had taken for him to bustle the woman up to his room, had it been the work of days rather than weeks, hours rather than days, how efficient was he now in these matters. In my case it had been, I remembered, one week exactly.

The waiter brought our first courses, mine was a small mesclun salad topped with some very pale grated carrot, the vegetables flown in from some distant place and then transported by truck no doubt. There was nothing native about my plate and I felt depressed just contemplating it, these vegetables in the aridity of a landscape that allowed only for olives, prickly pears, it was my own fault for ordering the dish.

Meanwhile, Maria was calmly cutting into an extravagant plate of food, a lobster dish that had been set on the menu in what had seemed to me an unnecessarily complicated prose description, several lines at least, all of which was almost certainly intended to justify the inflated price that accompanied the dish, one of the most expensive on the menu. She was eating with relish, unlike my salad, her dish looked delicious, the meat rich and glossy, a lobster claw, partially disemboweled, rose out of the pile of meat and butter like an upraised fist.

It was hard not to be distracted by the sight of this woman, who ate her expensive dish with such deliberate pleasure. Perhaps she had every right to the little luxury, I might have been the one paying, but if Christopher had wronged her in some way—and how could he have not—wasn't it right that as his wife, I should pay recompense? I waited for her to continue and wondered if she had sat in this restaurant, perhaps at this very table, with Christopher. She might have ordered the same lobster appetizer, he would have appealed to her appetite, to her desire for carnal satisfaction, encouraging her to be expansive.

Once a woman is behaving in a way that is other to herself, once she is acting in a manner out of the ordinary, unlikely things become possible, and that is half the task of seduction. Perhaps now, as she sucked the meat out of the lobster's claw, her chin growing slick with butter, she was reliving her own seduction, to which my presence was a mere ancillary. As if her emotions had been softened by the succulent dish, she began to speak of Christopher, without anger, almost dreamily. I thought he was very handsome, she said, men don't look like him around here. His manner was completely different too, he was always laughing, most of the time I didn't know what he was laughing at, but there was nothing mean about his laughter, I never felt like he was laughing at me.

All the women in the hotel were instantly attracted by him, she continued, from the moment he arrived they were talking about how handsome he was, how sexy—this was embarrassing and I averted my gaze, it was as if a girlfriend had referred to my own father as sexy, the word sounded jejune coming out of her mouth, so childish as to be utterly divorced from the act of sex itself—everyone had noticed that he had come alone, very few men come to the hotel alone, and none as young and handsome as he.

She lowered her eyes modestly to her plate, where they contemplated the ruin of the lobster dish. She had made short work of it. I never expected that he would notice me, she continued, of all the women working at the hotel. I hadn't noticed so many female staff at the hotel, the way she said it you would have thought there were absolute hordes, all of whom she had succeeded in beating off with a stick, but in any case I got the point, I understood that Christopher was a trophy. But, she continued, he took an interest, he kept stopping by, whenever I was working he would come and talk to me, he was obviously a busy man but he seemed to have plenty of time.

Christopher is always very good at finding time for the things he is interested in.

I tried to sound neutral, I wanted to keep my bitterness out of the conversation, but she barely seemed to notice that I had said anything at all, she continued almost without pause. And he was so interesting, I can say with my hand on my heart—she did pause this time, to lift her hand and place it on her bosom, which heaved with emotion, a gesture I thought Christopher would have found endearing, even enchanting, for all its apparent gaucheness—that I had never met such an intelligent man in my life. This was hardly surprising, the bar did not seem to be set especially high, Stefano, for all his merits, was not obviously an intellectual force.

But that was unkind. As the waiter took our plates away—mine still bearing a large portion of the salad, Maria's wiped clean—she continued. He knew about so many things, but he talked about them in a way that didn't make you feel bad or small, he wasn't an arrogant type, even if he had so many privileges. Here, she paused to look at me, as much to say that I, on the other hand, had been ossified by my privilege. I nodded grimly and ordered another glass of wine for both of us, she had nodded in a cursory, almost dismissive way when I asked if she would care for a second. After a moment, she added, Christopher is a gentleman, I saw that at once.

All right, I said, Yes, I suppose you are right.

I almost laughed, it was an absurdity, he was no more real to her than a prince in a fairy tale, a hero from a novel, and this despite the fact that he had treated her badly. Still, as she continued to speak, I thought she must harbor hopes of holding him to account, I listened and waited for her to reach the point, the reason why she had asked to sit down in the first place. But this seemed to elude her, and as she continued to tell me about Christopher's virtues, about his appealing manner, his kindness, without going into any detail about what had actually taken place between them, I thought again that perhaps nothing had happened, she had simply fallen in love with him, his small and rather nonspecific attentions having been enough.

She was younger than I had initially thought, perhaps as young as nineteen or twenty, a mere child, with a child's audacity. The waiter brought our main courses, she had ordered the steak, the most expensive entrée on the menu, I suppose once I had invited her to dine with me, she had thought she ought to make the most of it.

How old are you? I asked abruptly.

Twenty. My birthday was in August.

She said this with some pride, perhaps because twenty was a milestone, you were no longer a teenager once you reached that age. Or perhaps the pride came from the fact that she was so much younger than me, she must have been aware of what that was worth.

And Christopher, he was more than twice her age. Of course, at twenty girls do not care so much about age, a woman of thirty would think twice before embarking on an affair with a man more than two decades older, should the affair develop into something more serious—and the odds of a woman wishing for it to become something serious grew exponentially as she aged—

then a gap of two decades would become critical, nobody wanted to marry a man who would soon be at death's door.

But death is still abstract when you are twenty. The age difference would have meant nothing to Maria, this was possibly why men were attracted to women who were so much younger than they were. They made them feel young not because of their own youthful bodies, but because they were incapable of perceiving the meaning of their lovers' aging flesh. The body of a forty- or even fifty-year-old man is not always so dramatically different from the body of a twenty-five-year-old—for this, we have the wonders of diet and personal trainers to thank—but the differences are nonetheless there, it is only that a woman needs to be of a certain age in order to understand their true meaning.

And for this understanding, I thought, Maria was too young. She chewed on her steak and then, almost reluctantly, began to ask me questions about Christopher. I realized that this was what she had sat down to do—to ask me about my husband, to learn more about the man who had captured both her hope and affections. But I also saw that it was difficult for her, in doing so she was ceding ground to me as his wife, anything I said, even the fact that I could say anything at all, had the potential to devalue her experience of the man, which it was evident she wanted to safeguard.

And yet she needed to talk about him—for example, she was filled with the desire to say his name, I saw that it gave her a thrill, just pronouncing the three syllables, *Chris, to, pher,* which she did again and again, a sign that she was truly infatuated, when you are infatuated even speaking the name of the loved one is excitement enough. It had also been like that with me once, I had mentioned Christopher excessively in conversation, expounding on his views, his small acts and opinions (which at the time I had thought highly individualistic, I was a fool), it must have been very tedious for those around me.

And it was now no different with Maria. It was only her desire for more—of him, I think—that had led her to seek me out, she wanted to know everything about him, no detail could be too mundane, even if the source from which she acquired this information was inherently troubling. She was willing to pay the price for that information. But at the same time, her desire was fragile, too specific, she did not want to know anything that might disrupt the fantasy she had created in her head. She began asking questions, very basic ones, where had Christopher grown up, did he have siblings, did he like animals, dogs, for example, did he like dogs, he was always carrying books, did he really enjoy reading so much?

Her questions were careful to exclude the life

we had together—she never asked, for example, how we had met, where we lived, or if we had children, that was a dead zone as far as she was concerned—the entire exercise had been devised in order to allow her to elaborate on the image she already had of Christopher. Toward whom she appeared to feel no anger, despite the fact that he had upset her, reduced her to tears. I became more and more convinced that nothing concrete had taken place between them, she seemed to me more like a love-struck teenager than a scorned lover, a teenager was very nearly what she was.

But of course, it is possible to be both. We finished our dishes—although she did much of the talking, often talking over my responses to the very questions she was so keen to ask, she had eaten her steak with impressive rapidity, I was much slower to eat my plate of pasta. My answers were not especially illuminating, I was reluctant to say anything that might hurt her, she was a child after all. And although what she wanted was information about Christopher, the more I assented to her demand, the greater the reality of our marriage, the more painful the evidence of its history.

At one point she stayed her barrage of questions in order to say, with a nod at my plate, The pasta is not good here, you should have ordered something simple, they try to cook in the Italian way but it is not their strength, they don't do it well. I nodded, she spoke in an admonishing tone of voice, doing so appeared to give her some small pleasure, I didn't think it worth saying that I would have thought a salad and a plate of pasta were simple enough, as she was obviously correct and had managed to eat much better than I had, although, I couldn't help but notice, at far greater expense.

I stood up without asking if she would like coffee or a dessert. It was childish but I had taken umbrage, it was something about the peremptory manner in which she had criticized my order— advice that came too late, her words would have been more useful at the outset, when we had been ordering our food for example. Of course, I knew even then that it wasn't her order or the meal that I was going to pay for. This was all just a cipher for another infraction, whether she had intended to or not she had flaunted what was, at the very least, a flirtation between her and my husband, and she had done it as though I had no right to feel in any way nonplussed.

Perhaps from her perspective I did not, if I couldn't keep my husband, that was my own fault, or some such logic. Or, more likely, the notion of my discomfort simply hadn't occurred to her, she did not strike me as the most empathetic of women and she was still young, she lacked a certain kind of imagination. That would eventually be forced upon her. She sat and stared at me a moment, as if surprised that I hadn't suggested coffee or a dessert. However, I was stubborn, I did not intend to feed this woman any longer, there was a brief standoff and then she relented and stood up.

As she accompanied me through the lobby, I asked, and I don't know now where I found the nerve to pose such a direct and essentially ill-mannered question, So did you sleep with him or not?

I suppose I asked because I was certain that she would say no, not out of any instinct for denial, because for all her insensitivities she struck me as an honest woman, honest to a fault, but because it now seemed clear to me that, after all, nothing of substance had taken place between them. Once she denied the charge, I would simply apologize for the question, anyway I was a foreigner, capable of speaking all forms of rude madness.

But she did not deny it. Instead she blushed, her entire face changing shade. At first I thought it was her modesty, the question was abrupt and none too subtle, perhaps she was affronted, it was more evidence of my erratic personality, Christopher might have complained of it, it was not surprising that he was running away from his hysterical and irrational wife—but then, why would Christopher have mentioned me at all? She was still flushed when she spoke, but her voice and manner were very calm, her high color was the only giveaway, the only indication that something was wrong.

Yes. Of course, I knew he was married, she said, her color deepening further as she said the words, which she must have known were damning. I saw the ring, as he was checking in.

For a moment, I was too stunned to reply. I felt a wave of unexpected anger that was without clear object—I could hardly blame this girl, or even Christopher, they were perfectly within their rights to do as they wished. Still, I found it difficult to look at the girl, I swallowed and averted my gaze.

You saw his ring?

Of course Christopher would have slept with this girl, I should have known this all along. The fact that he was wearing his wedding ring was more surprising, I thought, the idea that Christopher would have dug out his ring and taken to wearing it, just as the marriage itself was irrevocably collapsing, was almost unbelievable. But Maria interpreted the inflection in my voice to be accusatory, she blushed again, even deeper, but continued in her calm, measured voice, I saw his ring, yes, I saw it.

The questions that should have followed, that she might reasonably have expected—questions as to the how and the when, the how many times, not to mention either anger or jealousy or most probably both, a coherent response to the news of your husband's adultery—did not come. Instead, as we stood in the lobby, I continued to ask her about the ring, as if in order to not ask about the sex she'd had with Christopher, my husband, what kind of a ring had he been wearing, did she notice?

She shrugged and looked uncomfortable.

Silver, very plain.

Was it thin? Or thick?

Not too thick. Perhaps—

She indicated a width of about half a centimeter. It was hardly decisive but it sounded like Christopher's wedding ring, or at least it didn't not sound like it. There might have been a perfectly logical, practical reason for which Christopher had put on the simple platinum ring. He might have put it on in the way that single women sometimes wore a ring in order to give the impression of unavailability, so that they might avoid unwanted attention and harassment, the flash of metal on the finger was often enough to dissuade even an arduous admirer.

Of course, unavailability served a different purpose for a man, or at least a man like Christopher. For him, perhaps, the ring served to give him a longer leash, it was more difficult to make demands of a married man, however far things went, he could always say, You knew from the start that I was married, you knew what you were getting into, it was plain as the ring on my finger. Perhaps each time he set out to roam—and I knew there had been plenty such times, over the course of our short marriage—he had dug out his wedding ring, in order to feel more free. From the drawer in his desk, or from the leather case in which he kept his watches and billfold clips, I realized then that I didn't even know where he kept his ring.

My breathing had grown regular again. But it was not nothing. I didn't know that it would ever be nothing—what person contemplates the details of her betrayal without feeling some combination of regret and humiliation, however far in the past? Abruptly, I wished Maria good night. I said that it was probably good-bye, although perhaps I would see her in the morning. I was aware that I was distracted, my behavior was not appropriate to the situation. She shrugged, she did not say whether or not she was working the next day. I noticed that she did not thank me for dinner, I hadn't expected her to, but I cared enough to take notice. The entire thing had been unpleasant, disconcerting, it was not an experience I hoped or expected to repeat, a tête-à-tête with a mistress of Christopher's. She stood with her hands in the pockets of her uniform and watched as I retreated, up the stairs, to my room.

7.

Christopher's body was found in a shallow ditch outside one of the villages inland, ten miles from the stone church I had visited the previous day. The place was perhaps five minutes from the nearest house by foot, and the road did not see very much traffic. The air of desertion was compounded by the fact that the area had been especially damaged in the fires, all the vegetation burnt to the ground. The body was found resting on dirt that had the color and texture of soot. When they lifted it, a fine powder coated its surface.

The body had been there at least overnight, perhaps longer. Although his wallet had been emptied of its cards and cash, it was not difficult for the police to identify him. Later, we would find that many hundreds of dollars had been removed from his accounts, and that mysterious charges had been made to his credit cards, charges that would later be reversed by fraud protection services, although it seemed beside the point, the man to whose accounts the companies were issuing these credits could not care, he would never open another bank or credit card statement.

He had been mugged and killed, a stupid and

anonymous death that could have taken place anywhere—in Manhattan or in London or Rome, there was nothing specific about the nature of his murder, the motivations were both familiar and banal, hardly worthy of notice—and there was something ignominious not only in the fact of his body lying abandoned in a ditch, but in the notion that he had traveled so far, to this foreign landscape and culture, only to confront a death that could have taken place one block from his own apartment in London.

In the first stunned hours after I was informed of his death—when the police arrived at the hotel I was in my room packing to leave, Kostas had already called the driver who had brought me from Athens to Mani and he was due to arrive shortly, of course there was no journey to Athens that day, the driver had likely traveled some distance in order to pick me up from the hotel, a costly inconvenience, but nobody mentioned the matter, this is precisely the kind of thing that people do not bother you about, when there has been a death in the family—my mind remained fixed on this small point, the inappropriateness of his death, its small and even accidental quality.

A friend used to say, in speaking of her ex-boyfriends (and later three ex-husbands, she was an eternal optimist), He's dead to me, a phrase I did not especially like, it sounded too violent for what is essentially a regular occurrence, the break-down of a relationship. My friend did not look as if she were capable of thinking such vicious and decisive thoughts, much less feeling them, but she always assured me that there was real sentiment behind the words. Of course, it was only a turn of phrase, but I was always too superstitious to say such a thing, *he's dead to me,* it felt like bad karma, although I don't believe in karma.

And yet, despite my caution, I was the one now living out this macabre phrase, which wasn't even my own, *he's dead to me.* The situation was one you sometimes imagine—in moments of extreme love or hate, in the grip of either fear or fantastical loathing—but which you do not believe to be actually possible. Even when you stand at the altar and declare *until death do us part,* death remains abstract, something that caps a long and happy life together, two elderly people holding hands, grandchildren and a cottage by the sea. But there were no children or grandchildren in this case, no countryside retreat, there was barely a marriage at all, only something between the two phrases, *he's dead to me* and *until death do us part.*

As soon as I hung up the phone, I left the room and went down to the lobby, Kostas had only said that there had been a terrible accident involving Christopher, at that point I didn't yet know the full extent of what had occurred.

Kostas and the two police officers standing beside him lowered their heads as I approached. A certain respect is accorded to a woman who is about to be informed of her husband's untimely death, and it dawned on me then that Christopher was dead. Kostas introduced the officers from the local station, unfortunately there had been some very bad news.

Kostas continued, translating for the officers, who spoke without looking at me, apart from the occasional surreptitious glance, perhaps they were sizing me up, they might have been looking for suspects and the first suspect is always the wife or husband, everybody knows that. But as Kostas continued to translate for the men, and I listened, numb, to their words, which I could not comprehend, I decided it wasn't suspicion but mere awkwardness that was coloring their response, nobody likes to be the bearer of bad news and they had no way of gauging how I might respond, whether or not there would be rage or hysterics or total disbelief, no, I didn't blame them at all.

I assumed that Kostas had been told at least some of the particulars in advance. Nonetheless, as each piece of information was relayed to him, he gave a little gasp before turning to me with a more subdued expression and telling me that, for example, my husband's body had been found by the side of the road, that he had been hit on the back of the head, likely with a rock or other blunt instrument, that it looked like a mugging. Perhaps he thought surprise was appropriate, it was a difficult tone to strike, somewhere between sympathetic dismay and bureaucratic vacancy, he was only transmitting the message.

I must have been in a state of shock. I kept nodding, as piece by piece the disaster continued to unfold before me, I asked how long he had been dead and they said they did not know necessarily, that would only come out in the autopsy, but not long, the body was—Kostas stopped, he wore an expression of consternation, as if reluctant to relate what followed—still relatively fresh and undisturbed, apart from the wound at the back of his head, there had not been very much decay. So he had died in the last day, while I was here, at the hotel? The police shook their heads, again, they could not say for certain until they received the coroner's report but certainly he could not have been there for very long, the area was full of wild animals, the body would not have been as pristine as it was, he looked, they said, almost like he was sleeping.

Apart from the wound at the back of his head. A large patch of blood, the likes of which would never be seen on the head of a sleeping man, it hardly made sense to describe him as such. And yet it might have been as they said—perhaps when the body was found he was lying on his back, the blood concealed, the eyes closed, could his eyes have closed in death, was it possible that when he was found his eyes were not staring out in horror, the unexpected fact of his death, but were indeed closed, his face peaceful? Like a man who had decided to lie down in the road, a man who had fallen asleep on the asphalt.

Can you go with them now?

I looked at Kostas blankly, I had lost the thread of what he was saying. Where? I said stupidly. He said, To the police station, to identify the body, they need someone to identify the body. Of course, I said, I just need to get my things, there is a phone call I need to make. I needed to tell Isabella—the moment they said the words confirming Christopher's death it was already too late, by that point she should have already known. Isabella was the person who should be here, Isabella the one to claim the body of her son, I was only—a former spouse, I realized belatedly, or near enough.

One of the officers cleared his throat impatiently, as if to say that they had waited long enough, there were limits to their sympathy and discretion. I said again that I only needed to go back to my room to gather a few things, one quick phone call and then I was free to go with them and they nodded. I intended to call Isabella from my room but as I stood by the side of the bed, I hesitated, the men were waiting downstairs, it was hardly the work of a minute or two. I didn't know what I would say, I couldn't imagine the words—Isabella, I have some very bad news, Isabella, something terrible has happened.

It would have been easier if I had been crying, I thought, hysterical. Isabella would have told me to calm down, to get hold of myself, she would have put herself in the false position of being in control, when she was not, when neither of us was, any longer, in control of anything. I waited a moment longer and then I did not call her, I said to myself that I would leave her a few last hours, during which her world remained coherent, still rational, both an act of kindness and an act of cruelty, she would have wanted to know at once, we all would have.

When I returned to the lobby, one of the men had disappeared and Kostas stood beside the remaining police officer. Kostas told me as we departed that the police would arrange for a car to take me back to the hotel. Or perhaps one of the officers would drive me, but in any case I should not hesitate to contact him if I needed anything. He gave me a card with his mobile phone number written on it. Then he said that he assumed I would no longer be leaving that day, and offered to call the airline to cancel my ticket, he assured me that there would be no difficulty, a death in the family.

I thanked him and hurried after the officer, who

was already leaving. As we exited the hotel I saw that the car was waiting, the other officer was behind the wheel and the engine was running. We got inside. The first officer insisted that I sit in the front passenger seat while he sat in the back of the car, alone, like a junior partner. Perhaps he worried that if I sat in the back while the two officers sat in front it would look too much like they had arrested me and I was being brought in for questioning, already as we drove through the interior people were stopping to watch, peering into the windows of the car as if I were a criminal.

But as I sat in the front of the car, the officer beside me driving in silence, the officer in the back staring at the headrest before him or occasionally staring out the window, it was not guilt that I felt. Nor did I yet feel grief. I felt only a sense of incredulity, that this had befallen us, something I could never have imagined, something that was at once entirely possible (it had happened, so it must be) and yet still experienced as impossible, the impossible thing that had somehow came to pass, *some stammer in the divine speech*.

At the same time, one part of my mind was preoccupied with the practicalities, of which there were bound to be many, and of which I knew I was not the correct executor. I would need to tell someone—although not these officers, within the domain of the law I was still his wife and there was something shameful about airing the confused state of our marriage to these strangers, in this moment—that I was in a false position, not exactly an impostor but nonetheless operating under false pretenses. In short, I would need to tell Isabella. About the separation, the true state of affairs between her son and me. And then it would fall to her, the funeral arrangements, the transportation of the body, whatever else needed to be arranged.

The police car pulled into the station, a single-story concrete building, there were dogs outside but they were chained, intimidating animals, it was easy to imagine them lunging and snapping at the end of their leashes. As the car slowed, I saw the officers turn to look at me. I averted my gaze, I felt myself to be playing the part of the grieving widow—a sensation that, had I genuinely been a grieving widow, I never would have felt, there was a small but definite wedge pushing between the person I was and the person I was purporting to be.

One of the officers ran to open the car door for me. I stepped out, the sky was overcast again and I wondered if it would rain. The officers motioned for me to follow them into the station, a building so small that I wondered where they could be keeping the body, whether there was enough room for a morgue. I followed the officers inside, in their extreme politesse they were

144

behaving as if I were an oversized ship being steered into a narrow port, waving their hands like air traffic controllers. They wore a general expression of anxiety and would be relieved when I was no longer their responsibility, when I was finally taken off their hands.

Inside, the station was near empty, there were a couple posters on the wall—I couldn't decipher their message, they were written in Greek and the images themselves were opaque. The overhead lights blinked irregularly. I was hurried through the waiting area, there were two rows of plastic chairs with seats that had warped over time, all empty, although it couldn't be that the area was without incident, the fires alone must have generated so many cases (missing persons, unidentified bodies, grieving parties). I was shown into a small office, a man stood up to greet me, although there was not very much in the way of an introduction, he merely rose to his feet and indicated that I should sit down.

I sat down. He also returned to his seat and began flipping through various files, as if he were simultaneously very busy and also a little bored by the situation, in a way it was understandable. He must have had a great many responsibilities, and although the matters that brought the public into his office were necessarily of great individual concern, to him it was just another day's work, he couldn't be expected to live his life at a pitch of continual crisis, day after day, it was his job to remain calm, rational, he couldn't give way to his emotions.

Indeed, the entire atmosphere in the station was overwhelmingly sterile, nothing like what you might expect from watching police procedural shows on television, which are populated with colorful characters and extreme human dramas, there was nothing of the sort on display here. Eventually, the officer looked up at me and asked to see my passport, which luckily I had thought to bring, neither of the two officers had told me to bring identification of any kind. As I handed the passport to the officer I said, I didn't take his name when we married, I kept my own.

He nodded, perhaps this information wasn't relevant. He rose and said, holding the passport in one hand, that he would be back in a moment. I sat in the chair, I put my hands in the pockets of my jacket, I was reminded again that I had not called Isabella, that Isabella did not yet know that Christopher was dead. The reality of his death was everywhere around me, here in this room, and yet Isabella knew nothing of it, however material this new reality, it was not yet consistent, not yet pervasive. It had been a little more than an hour since the police had come for me. The officer returned, carrying both my passport and a laptop, which he opened and placed before me.

Here is your passport, he said. I thanked him, he pushed the laptop a couple inches away and sat down on the edge of the desk, he said that he would be showing me a number of photographs on the computer—he waved a hand in the direction of the laptop—from which I would identify the body. I understood this to mean that I would look at photographs of the body before proceeding to the body itself—as though the images were a form of preparation, the way a nurse practitioner swipes your arm with an alcohol swab before an injection, a ritual that only exacerbates your dread.

This seemed much worse and I told him I would rather proceed directly, I would rather just see the body. He shook his head, perhaps he thought his English was failing him. I apologized for not being able to speak his language and he shook his head again. He motioned to the laptop for a second time. Only the photos, he said, and then repeated, Only the photos. For a moment, I wondered if the body had been lost or destroyed or in some way compromised, only the photos remained—a furthering of the nightmare, conceived in an instant. Then I realized that he meant only that the photos would be used to identify the body, *only the photos,* the body itself would remain elsewhere.

He asked if I was ready to begin and I nodded. The situation was not what I had expected, how strange it was, that one could have expectations for a situation never before imagined, and yet it was the case. I had been prepared to see the body and now I would only see photographs of the body, something that felt insufficient, too slight for the gravity of the situation, he had died alone and now he would be alone in his death, unwitnessed by anything apart from the flash of a camera.

I could have wept, it was so appalling. The officer touched the keyboard, rousing the machine from sleep, there were almost no icons on the desktop, which still had the preset factory image as its wallpaper. He frowned as he clicked on a folder—I couldn't read the name of the folder, it was in Greek, it might have said *autopsies* or *ID* or simply *photos,* I had no idea—and then began scrolling through a surprising number of files, at least fifty or sixty. The task took some time, he started to hum tunelessly, his finger on the mouse pad.

Perhaps there had been many deaths in recent weeks, it wasn't impossible, people must have died in the fires, I dreaded to think what those photographs would look like. The officer made a little sound of satisfaction—at last, he had found what he was looking for—and then without further ado (he had, after all, already warned me) he clicked on the file and the screen was filled with an image of Christopher's face in death, his head resting on a metal surface, presumably the examining table at the coroner's office. I stared at the image, the officer was watching me, then he looked away, discreetly, as if to give me privacy. After a moment, he cleared his throat and I looked up, startled.

Well?

I looked back at the photograph. I didn't say anything—yes, of course it was Christopher, but I didn't recognize the man in the image, that is to say, it was and it was not Christopher. I had never seen him in such a state, one eye was half opened and the other closed (it turned out they were neither opened nor closed in death but both, and this seemed to me a terrible thing, that nobody had bothered to close the other eye) and his mouth hung open as if he were in a state of shock, the shock of his death, which had been unusually violent—Christopher was no more accustomed to violence than the rest of us, possibly even less so.

It was a face that did not often confront you in life: the unvarnished face of death, so different from the face of the dead as presented in funeral parlors or in death masks, a face that has been processed, to which the dignity has been restored, and from which the emotion has been washed. *He looked as if he were sleeping,* a common thing to say, an attempt to deny the finality of death, sleep being some intermediate state between being and nothing, presence and absence. But it was more than this, *he looked as if he were sleeping*—it was also, I now understood, an attempt to pretend that the journey into death, the process of dying, was in some way peaceful, when it was almost certainly not.

Christopher's face was not the face of a man sleeping, a man at peace. It was the face of a man who had been afraid. All faces are made stupid by fear, the emotion overrides intelligence, charm, humor, kindness, the qualities by which we know people, and for which we fall in love. But who is not afraid in the face of death? It was for this reason I was unable to say at once and definitively, This is Christopher, it was and it was not, the expression was unrecognizable and even the features themselves did not look like they belonged to the man I had been married to for five years, the man I was still married to.

The officer leaned forward, he clicked on the folder again. I had not responded to his question, he must have thought I needed to see more photographs in order to identify my husband, as if that single image was not enough, perhaps in some cases it was not—as I'd just seen, death transformed the face beyond recognition. I raised my hand to stop him, I didn't need to see anything more, it was evidently Christopher, or rather, the sense I had that it was not—that it was a doppelgänger, a visual illusion, something other— would not be dispelled by further photographs.

It's him, I said. That is Christopher.

I said *it* and *that* rather than *he,* people often do, the sentence *He is Christopher* sounded unnatural, it was impossible to pronounce. Nor was it reflective of the truth, there had been no *he,* there was nothing substantial to what I had seen, simply a collection of pixels, a file on the laptop. I had no desire to see the body and yet I could not believe that I was not going to see the body. I suddenly felt that I should at least ask. I raised my voice and said, Where is the body? I could not say, Where is he, it sounded like denial but in fact was almost acceptance, or at least an affirmation of the fact that once a death has occurred, the person is departed and there is nothing left but the body, *it* and not *he,* a mere semblance of the living person.

The officer—who lifted his hands from the computer as soon as I spoke, as if he too had no desire to look at any more images and was relieved, it might have been his job but that didn't necessarily mean that he enjoyed the process— shrugged. The body is next door, he said. The phrase *next door* sounded too casual for such a serious thing, the location of my husband's body. Next door, I repeated, the body is next door, Christopher is next door? And he shrugged again, waving his arm in the general direction of the hall, as if Christopher's body had no concrete location, as if it were only out there, moving from place to place, traveling from room to room.

He asked, Do you wish to see the body? The question took me by surprise, although it shouldn't have—of course such a thing would be offered to the wife, the widow, particularly one who had inquired after the location of the body, who had been so surprised to be confronted with photographs rather than the thing itself—and I hesitated, it was not that I was squeamish, although there was that too, seeing the photographs had been bad enough. It was more that I wondered if I had the right, if there was a woman—it's always a woman at the side of the body, Mary Magdalene, Antigone, Lady Capulet, woman in multiple guises—who should have been there instead of me, perhaps Isabella, perhaps someone else.

Christopher had gone. What happened now| was private to himself—*as there are apartments in our own minds that we never enter without apology, we should respect the seals of others*—and what was more private than one's death, particularly when it was violent or unnatural? Wasn't that why photographs of bodies torn from crime scenes and car accidents struck us as so tasteless, why we despised ourselves when we could not help but rubberneck at a car accident, the feet (still shod) sticking out from under the blue tarp? It wasn't simply the horror of the dead body, it was the invasion of a stranger's privacy, the act of seeing what should not be seen.

How could I know whether Christopher would have wanted to be seen by me, in this state—his eyes askew, his mouth propped open, he was a vain man, he had a sense of propriety, even the thought of such a death would have humiliated him—how could I know what I had been to him, in the final moments before his death? And yet he needed to be seen, by someone. I had not yet called Isabella, she would not arrive until tomorrow at the earliest, by which point the body would have been dead forty-eight hours or longer, in some state of partial decomposition, hardly a sight for an elderly woman, however stern her moral fiber—no, the body could not go unseen for so long.

Yes, I said to the officer, who looked up, as if in surprise, I would like to see the body, and he nodded and reached into his pocket and withdrew a set of keys.

8.

Among Christopher's things was an old copy of the *London Review of Books*, from June of that year. This was hardly surprising, back issues of this and other publications accumulated everywhere in our apartment, the bathroom was overflowing with issues that were as old as a year. That particular issue of the *London Review* had several interesting articles, which I think Christopher would have enjoyed and no doubt had read—he had brought the issue all the way to Greece, perhaps he had even read it on the plane.

In general, he had with him a considerable array of reading material, a suitcase full of books, journals, notebooks, papers. He must have been intending to stay in Greece for some time, perhaps he genuinely had hoped to finish his book during this trip. At that point, I had not yet gone into his computer, opening the files, looking through documents, checking to see if there was anything that might be publishable, at the behest of his agent and editor and Isabella too—she was, of course, to be involved in all of this. I had been reluctant, postponing the task, from the start I had suspected that it would be an unsettling experience, like prying into the mind, the private thoughts of the dead.

When I finally did sit down in front of the machine—a familiar object, I had seen it daily when we were living together—I was reminded of how abrupt and unnatural death always is, at least as we experience it: always an interruption, always things that are left unfinished. This was manifested in Christopher's laptop, the desktop was covered in an intricate mosaic of files and documents, there were at least a hundred different and sometimes oddly named folders—*other people's work, internet.* You name a folder without thinking, there are obvious names for some—*accounts, articles*—but others have the quality of junk drawers, you hardly remember their contents, you never imagine that one day someone else would be rummaging through them. And yet I was now doing precisely this. In amongst the junk drawers, as I hunted for the documents that Isabella and the agent and the editor all insisted were there—a partial manuscript, nearly complete, which unbeknownst to me Christopher had promised to deliver within the next six months, a deadline that passed shortly after his death, an uncanny affirmation of a lie I had told Isabella, about Christopher's work and the near completion of his book, a lie that had somehow come true or at the very least been reiterated by Christopher himself—I found other things. Things that presumably Christopher would never have wished for me to see: for example, a folder filled with pornographic pictures he had downloaded from the Internet.

On the surface there was nothing too painful to discover, he did not have a penchant for a particularly violent kind of fetish porn, nor was he collecting gay erotica or visiting sites called Black Beauties or Hot Asian Anal. I had heard such stories, which in the end were stories about a single realization, the understanding that you had never fulfilled or even addressed the secret desire, the most vividly imagined fantasies, of your partner. That you had never been, on some level, what he or she had been looking for, your partner's mind always elsewhere or making do, something that cast the record of your sexual encounters into a paltry and humiliating light, he had always been trying not to see you, not as you actually were.

There was nothing like that. And yet I remained tense, I clicked on maybe four or five JPEGs before I closed the folder, heart pounding. The images were not even particularly lewd, given that they were pornographic, nor were they especially personal—pornography proves the generalized nature of desire, it appeared that Christopher had the same desires as many other men, a predilection for threesomes, blow jobs, that sort of thing. Several of the files I opened contained images of two women, but it was hardly very shocking, on the contrary, it was a predilection I already knew firsthand.

Most of the images were meant to look like what in England had once been called Readers' Wives—that is to say, amateur photographs of ordinary people—but which had now become the predominant aesthetic of Internet pornography. The quality of the photographs was poor, the lighting was harsh and unflattering, the setting had the crude luxury particular to the suburbs, large living rooms furnished with pleather sofas and glass-and-steel furniture. And the girls, while pretty, could hardly be mistaken for ordinary porn stars, they wore very little makeup and there was no visible enhancement to their figures.

Still, they were clearly at ease in front of the camera. They behaved as if they were professionals, that was a function of the age we lived in, people took photographs of themselves all day long, in every act and situation, eating their breakfast, sitting on the train, standing in front of the mirror. The effect was not a new candidness or verisimilitude to the photographs that proliferated—on our phones, computers, on the Internet—but rather the opposite: the artifice of photography had infiltrated our daily lives. We pose all the time, even when we are not being photographed at all.

Two of the photographs—neither professional nor amateur but something in between—featured a woman who was stark naked except for a pair of knee-high sports socks. I would not have thought that socks were especially Christopher's thing, but the girl was young and attractive. In one photograph, she sat on the edge of a chair with her legs wide apart, she had thrown her head back and her mouth was open, as if she were in a state of ecstasy. In the second photograph, she cupped her breasts with both hands while leaning forward, her mouth was still open but in a manner that was more pragmatic, there was only one thing really to do with such a mouth, and that was to put something in it.

Both poses had been replicated thousands or possibly millions of times, the Internet was over-flowing with pictures of women in those exact positions, even their facial expressions would be identical—but I knew that was no impediment to stimulation and arousal, in general one doesn't worry too much about clichés when in the grips of or seeking excitation. Christopher must have masturbated to these images—what else was pornography for, why else would he have taken the trouble to download these images, if not for reliable titillation?

But perhaps it was not so obvious or forlorn a scenario as that, Christopher hunched before the computer, his face illuminated by the light of the screen. Perhaps these images had led to arousal that was then fulfilled with a living, breathing partner, a woman or perhaps two, waiting in the bedroom or maybe looking at the computer with him, at one point, it might even have been me. A woman with whom he would then proceed: the pornographic image still fixed in his imagination, a supplement to the living and breathing body, which in itself was no longer enough, the live sex that followed always something of a disappointment compared to the limitless promise of the pornographic fantasy, the boundlessness of the Internet.

But I only went into his computer weeks, months later, whereas the June issue of the *London Review of Books* I saw perhaps only a few days after his death, or rather, after I was informed of his death. By that point Isabella had arrived. I had called her from the police station, after I had seen Christopher's body, laid out on a steel table, the entire thing covered with a sheet, including the face. This unnerved me yet further, although there was no reason why I should have expected the body to be arranged any differently, for the sheet to be drawn up to the shoulders for example, as if he were lying in bed, *he looked as if he were sleeping.*

He did not look as if he were sleeping. His face, when the police officer drew the sheet back, was fixed in the same expression as I had seen in the photographs—again, a trick of the imagination, which is always stupid and slow in such situations,

I had thought his face would be different, look different, but it was exactly as in the photographs, the eyes askew, the mouth propped open. And yet the wound at the back of his head, with its black crust of blood, was larger and more open than I had expected, it seemed to be ongoing, as if it were continuing to cause distress, as if he were still experiencing pain, right there in front of me.

I turned away from the table. As he drew the sheet up again, the police officer said he assumed the body would be shipped back home rather than buried or cremated here in Greece. I nodded, although in truth I did not know, I had not the least idea what Christopher would have wanted, I could not believe he would have wanted anything at all. You will need to inform the embassy, the body will need to be embalmed, the sooner the better, the police officer said. There are procedures. I nodded again and said that as soon as Christopher's mother arrived we could proceed, and he turned away, satisfied.

He did not ask why it required Isabella's arrival, perhaps to him, this deference to the mother seemed only natural. At any rate, she arrived soon enough. Isabella and Mark took the first flight out of London, the very next morning. Isabella's manner, when I called her from the police station, was strangely calm. She said, Oh no, and then was silent for so long that I thought she must have fainted. I said her name several times and then

160

Mark took the phone and I had to say it again, Christopher has been found dead, he is dead. In the background, I could hear Isabella sobbing, a low and terrible sound. I pressed my hand to my mouth. There was a thud, as if she had collapsed to the ground. I closed my eyes. I'm going to have to call you back, Mark said, I will call you back.

Less than twenty-four hours later, I stood at the hotel gate as the car drove up, Mark and Isabella sitting frozen in the back. They must have instructed the driver to make good time, it was only a little past noon. When she got out of the car Isabella did not look at me but looked around her, at the road, then up at the hills and the sky, as if trying to understand what had drawn her son to this place. I watched her from the gate, one hand shielding my eyes from the glare of the sun. The temperature was dropping by the day, I saw that Isabella and Mark were wearing light coats, they had clearly checked the weather forecast before packing, despite their distress. Nevertheless, the sun was still bright.

At first, Isabella seemed to look at the landscape around her with an expression of bemusement—the mystified expression with which a beautiful wife confronts the face of a vulgar mistress, the face of her betrayal—but gradually I realized she was looking not with wonder but with hatred, the same enmity the wife always comes to feel for the mistress. She would hate this place for the rest of her life, until the day she died. As I stepped forward with my hands outstretched—we embraced, but cautiously, as though we were both incalculably fragile—I understood that although she had always hated me, her hatred had now dissipated and found another object. I had taken him away from her but never completely, not like this.

Almost the first thing she said, once she had been shown to her room and the door had closed behind us (she had sent Mark out on a mission, obviously invented, to the local chemist, she claimed to be suffering from upset stomach, from nausea, motion sickness from the drive), was, Why did he come here? She was standing by the window, Kostas had put Isabella and Mark in a suite, although not the one that Christopher had occupied. I looked at her, I couldn't remember the last time we had been alone with each other. She looked back at me, for a moment it was as if the primary relationship were between us, the men having died or been sent away. Perhaps now that was true.

I don't know, I said. I didn't find him in time, I was too late.

She shook her head, the muscles around her mouth tightened. It would have been about a woman, Christopher never could keep his cock in his pants.

I was stunned, I had never heard her use such

vulgar language and I had never heard her speak about her son in such aggressive and critical terms. She spoke not as if he had died but as though he had merely run away, as if she would be giving him a lecture upon his eventual return, I saw that she was in a state of complete denial.

She stood by the window, she was staring out at the water with a fixed expression, a woman filled with rage, at the situation, at the place, at the fact of her son's death, which she could not accept. At her son, who'd had the audacity to die on her, to put her in the unnatural position of outliving her only child, the nightmare of every mother. It was horrifying to look at her face, which had collapsed beneath the grief she was unable to directly express, I was entirely sympathetic to her predicament, and yet as she continued to speak, I wished she would stop.

I think nowadays they call it sex addiction. Men who can't stop chasing women, even when they are making fools of themselves. It gets worse with old age, you know. There's nothing worse than a panting old man. Of course, you must take some responsibility for the situation, she said. But I don't blame you, I know my son, I'm not sure that any woman would have been able to keep him from straying.

Her eyes suddenly filled with tears, as if she were speaking not of her son's infidelity but of his death—that was what she was really talking

163

about, and she was right, no woman could have kept him from dying. Things must have been strained between you, Christopher never said a word but I felt it. She paused. If only Christopher hadn't had reason to come to this place.

He came here, I said, to do research, to finish his book.

Isabella shook her head sharply. The book was only the excuse, she said, Christopher was never serious about his work. He was always running away. He always had somewhere to go, he made his life very busy. I think he was worried that if he stopped, he would realize that his life was empty.

This was unfair—although she loved him to excess, Isabella had never been able to take her son seriously. Now that he was dead, she would never have to acknowledge the depth of his ambitions, the fact that in death he had left things undone. She was not looking at me. I said that he had been close to finishing his manuscript (a lie), that I had read whole chapters (another lie), that in fact there was a critical link (even the phrase sounded false) in the book that could be made through the research he had been doing here in the southern Peloponnese.

Isabella did not respond, perhaps she did not hear me. Standing by the window, she looked like the saddest woman in the world. At any rate, she said, still looking out at the sea, you loved him. Despite his flaws. And that is something. He died loved. She did not look at me for affirmation—perhaps it was not even necessary, it was understood that I loved Christopher, what wife didn't love her husband? Even when her husband gave her sufficient cause not to? There was an appreciable pause, which Isabella seemed not to notice, before I said, Yes, Christopher was loved by many people, there is no doubt that he died loved.

But he was loved by you, she said insistently, the love of a wife is different, it's important.

More important than the love of his mother? I asked. I immediately regretted it, I would have taken the question back if I could, the woman's son had just died, if I could not be generous to her now, when would I? But she replied, somberly, Yes, it is the most important love, the love of the mother is a given, it is taken for granted. A child is born and for the rest of his or her life the mother will love the child, without the child doing anything in particular to earn it. But the love of a wife has to be earned, to be won in the first place and then kept.

She paused, and then added, although I thought without malice, You don't have children, perhaps it is difficult for you to understand. And I said in reply, Yes, I loved him, Isabella, he died loved, and she said, Ah. That's all I wanted to know.

And yet her words returned to me, as I went through Christopher's belongings, packing them up so that they could be taken back to London (the hotel staff had merely placed his things in boxes, they were in a state of total disarray, it was not a task I could have asked Isabella to perform. Isabella, whose grief had already taken precedence over mine, both because of her natural egotism and because the secret of my estranged status from Christopher meant that I did not believe my grief had any claims to make of its own, I allowed the situation to happen).

When I found the June issue of the *London Review of Books*, it was open to the back pages. Those pages contained personals and real estate listings—*colonial-style house on the coast of Goa, four kilometers from Monte San Savino, own wheels essential, life-enhancing writing holiday at luxury retreat.* In the bottom left-hand corner, on the page to which the issue was opened, the binding torn at the staples as if the pages had been folded back for some time,was a boxed ad that had been circled with apen, reading:

INFIDELITIES: Has life become some-what stale and routine? Would discreet dating introductions give you back that missing special spark?

Infidelities is all about the alternative relationship experience. We offer you a personal, professional, bespoke scheme, far removed from Internet searching.

Women are especially welcomed to our unique project. Please telephone James for a private friendly chat.

The ad went on to include both a landline and a mobile phone number. As I read it through a second time, I thought, somewhat mechanically, that the copywriter had no ear to speak of— why, for example, *somewhat stale* rather than simply *stale,* why *missing special spark* rather than *missing spark?* Perhaps it didn't matter in most circumstances but the ad had been placed in the *London Review of Books,* which had an educated and sophisticated readership, a readership who thought of itself that way. The tone of the advertisement was a complete mess, on the one hand it read like a proposal from a bank or an investment opportunity, for example there was the use of the word *scheme.* On the other hand it sounded like a badly conceived free-love experiment, why describe it as a *unique project,* why refer to it as *alternative?*

I smoothed the paper, my hands were trembling a little. It was the final line, the injunction to call James for a *private friendly chat,* that struck me as the most bizarre, particularly the inclusion of both a mobile and a landline number. I imagined this James, constantly on call, ready to drop everything should his telephone ring, either one, always prepared to enter into private and friendly conversation at any time of day or night, the more I thought about it the more the inconsistency of tone troubled me, on the one hand it was *professional, bespoke,* on the other hand it was a *chat,* it was *friendly.*

Christopher's agent was also called James, a charming and charismatic man in his sixties and a well-known figure in the publishing world, a man more different from this James could not be imagined. And yet perhaps the services they offered were not so dissimilar, discretion, sympathy, a kind of professional intimacy—I began to imagine Christopher's avuncular agent moonlighting as Infidelities James, writing the copy on his laptop, sending the form to the ad department of the *London Review*, waiting for the calls to come in, an absurd but nonetheless amusing image, perhaps it had been the echo of the name that had prompted Christopher to note the ad in the first place.

But what exactly was Infidelities offering to someone like Christopher, for example, who did not need any assistance in arranging his infidel-ities, or require any introductions—they happened to him, the way depression happened to some people—but who had nonetheless paused to note this ad? What could this scheme have provided? The kind of assistance Christopher would have needed was more in the management of his trysts and mistresses, an administrative service of some kind, orchestrating affairs was a headache, there were stories to be kept straight, diaries to be coordinated, evidence to be concealed.

Yes, Infidelities James would have had more luck if he'd advertised services that were more along these lines, that would have truly been *bespoke* (the advertisement was trying to give the impression of being upscale and sophisticated but in fact merely sounded suburban, essentially tawdry). Then Christopher might have stopped to pick up the telephone and say, Hello, I need help with my infidelities, more specifically, I need help managing them, they are becoming a bit of a headache. And then Infidelities James would have made a series of helpful suggestions or proposals, things that would smooth the poten-tially rough course of faithlessness, whether it was a second mobile phone or well-timed spousal gifts.

Above all, friendly and discreet as a priest, he would have condoned Christopher's faithlessness. And I knew then that this was the real reason Christopher had stopped to circle the advertisement. It didn't require a telephone call or a conversation with James, the mere fact of his advertisement and its brazen message was enough—there were others doing it, there were even people who wished to be unfaithful but did not know how. Christopher must have been reassured, he must have thought it was entirely natural, this compulsion of his, which had gone beyond pleasure and into something far more terrible. Toward the end, he had become like Moira Shearer in *The Red Shoes*, forced to dance, past pleasure or joy and into the realm of death.

How many had there been, exactly? *Christopher never could keep his cock in his pants.* I knew about three, for all our sakes I had pretended to myself and to him that it was only three, that it was a finite number. Three was bad enough for such a short marriage, three was infidelities, multiple affairs rather than an affair or two. And yet I had always known there had been others, possibly many others, *I don't blame you, I know my son, I'm not sure that any woman would have been able to keep him from straying.* Isabella had seen his faithlessness as a kind of cancer, for which the prognosis was always bad.

And which I had not succeeded in curing—I understood this now, and I understood that the coldness of her grief, the inexplicable and matter-of-fact vitriol she directed toward her son, would eventually find its true target. I pushed the paper away. Eventually Isabella would come to blame me, she was blaming me now, even if she didn't know it yet. My heart contracted—I could not think of anything to say in my defense. Christopher was dead, and I was living with another man, I had left him to his faithlessness—yes, in the end, I had been the one to do the leaving.

9.

Was that why, in the end, I did not tell Isabella and Mark that Christopher and I had separated—because of her question, concealed as a statement—*he died loved*—and because of the guilt, the obvious guilt of the living, which does not necessarily fade with time as promised? Even as early as that first visit to the police station, I already knew that I would not tell Isabella, that the moment to tell her would come and go, and I would not speak.

After I identified the body and was told I was free to go, when I stepped out of the police station, Stefano was waiting. The officer had ordered a car to take me back to the hotel. Stefano ran to open the car door, his face growing flushed, as if at the sight of me. When I reached the car he stopped and then gripped my hand in both of his, murmuring some words of condolence that I barely heard, perhaps *I heard about your husband* or *Such terrible news,* finally he lowered his head and said only that he was very sorry.

I nodded, I saw that he was in a strange position, caught between genuine sympathy—we were not friends, we had only spent a few hours together, and yet he was essentially empathetic, too human not to be able to imagine what I might be feeling—and some emotion that was more compromised, an expression of relief if not triumph. I did not yet suspect Stefano of greeting Christopher's death with happiness, I believed him to be a sensitive man, and the contemplation of death in anything but the abstract is difficult even for those who are not terribly sensitive.

And yet it was a solution of sorts, even in my stunned state I was able to see this, perhaps I even went so far as to think, At least someone will have benefited from this, there were upsides and downsides to everything, even the most extraordinary and unhappy events. I sat in the back of the car, I felt at once that Stefano was nervous, he did not know what to say, how to behave around the recently bereaved, unlike his great-aunt, he had no experience in the matter. I don't know what to say, I am shocked, he said.

I nodded, there was nothing to say in response to his comment, mostly I wished that he would stop talking. But he didn't. I happened to drive by the place where they found his body, he continued, I was working, the man I was driving was in a hurry, that road is the fastest route between the two villages. As he spoke, I covered my face with my hands. I had a headache, my face was hot. I don't know where the body was found, I said, they didn't tell me.

I didn't realize it was your husband, he hastened to add. The road was blocked and there was a police car, but I didn't see the body—unbidden, the image rose up, the legs under the tarp, the feet askew, he continued speaking—later I found out who it was, it was a shock, I had driven him a couple of times when he needed a car, he had been in the village for almost a month.

I lowered my hands. It was a moment of strange confirmation, I tried to remember what Stefano had said about Christopher—almost nothing, only that he knew I had been waiting for him. Certainly he had not said that Christopher had been a customer, that he had sat in the back of his car, like I had, as I was doing at that very moment. Still, hadn't I imagined Christopher riding in Stefano's car, occupying the space alongside me, the possible synchronicity merely unsettling? Now that Christopher was dead, the link between him and this man suddenly seemed more urgent, unwieldy with possible meaning.

Had Stefano driven Christopher before discovering that he had slept with Maria, or after, or both? Perhaps Christopher and Maria had arranged an inland tryst upon Christopher's return from Cape Tenaro—a strange location, but not impossible, a walk in the countryside after a drive—and Stefano had followed Maria there, seen evidence of the errant couple together, an enraging sight. And then, once Maria had reluctantly returned home, he might have leapt from the shadows to attack the man who had so carelessly upended his life—people lost their heads, there was some question as to whether it had been a blow designed to kill.

Stefano did not seem aware that he had said anything amiss. How many times had he driven him, I wanted to ask, and when most recently? Perhaps he had even picked up Christopher— Christopher, newly returned from the embrace of the unnamed woman in Cape Tenaro and already in search of another—outside the local bus station, although Christopher would never have taken the bus, the scenario was impossible. Stefano now looked up into the rearview mirror, he had felt that I was watching him.

I looked away. Perhaps Christopher had forgotten Stefano's name, or perhaps he had remembered and greeted him at the impossible bus station, having been reminded by Maria, she might have mentioned Stefano in a misguided attempt to make Christopher jealous, Christopher who, in my experience, did not get jealous. Perhaps Christopher had even telephoned him— a business card, passed along on an earlier journey—they might have made conversation as they drove, perhaps Christopher had told Stefano details of his trip, his excursion, what were to be his final days, about which none of us knew anything.

Stefano was looking at the road, he had long since fallen silent. This vision—or was fantasy the more honest word, I hardly knew—had left me winded, it suddenly seemed a mere indulgence of the imagination. If Stefano was guilty of this crime, of killing a man, would he have said to me—the widow, the person who should have been most concerned—that he had driven Christopher at all, would he have knit their two histories yet closer? Or perhaps it had been a nervous response, they say that the guilty sometimes wish to be apprehended.

He sat in the front of the car, suddenly an unknown quantity, a physical mass of potentialities. I sensed that he was a man capable of violence, but in itself that is nothing, most men are, and most women too. There was something terrible about falsely accusing a man of murder, even in the imagination. It was an act of speculation that contaminated everything, once seeded, doubt is almost impossible to dispel, I knew that already from my relationship with Christopher, the marriage had died at the hand of my imagination. Still, I could not help myself. I leaned forward and asked, When did you drive Christopher?

Early in his stay, only a couple times. He didn't use me again, I don't know why.

He replied promptly, his voice entirely natural, matter-of-fact. He spoke like a man who had nothing to hide and he said nothing further, he must have thought, The woman is in a state of shock, best to leave her alone, there is nothing to be said. I stared at the back of his neck, at his hands on the wheel, again I wondered what he was capable of and then I felt a wave of unguarded emotion. Whatever he did or did not do, his life had been derailed by Christopher's arrival. I again felt—it was impossible to deny, I recognized it at once—sympathy for the man. The same mechanism of destruction had operated upon my own life, it was something that we shared. I was silent, neither of us said anything further, until our safe arrival at the hotel.

Two mornings later, the day after Isabella and Mark's arrival, I met Isabella for breakfast. When I arrived, she was seated at a table on the far edge of the terrace, one with unimpeded views of the water. Her back was to me, her body was rigid, she looked like a statue or wood carving, entirely immobile, and although she must have been tired—when she turned, I saw that there were lines around her eyes and mouth, that her delicate face was puffed with strain—she also looked ageless, mummified by the force of her personality.

I hope I didn't keep you waiting.

After a long moment, she replied—No, you didn't, or It doesn't matter—and then slowly turned to face the table. I sat down across from her and ordered a coffee, I saw that her cup was already empty. The waiter asked if she would like another coffee. She nodded, without making eye contact. Only once the waiter had gone did she raise her head and look at me.

I want to apologize for my behavior yesterday. I should never have said those things about Christopher. Mark was very angry with me when I told him.

For a brief moment there was a ghost of coquetry in her manner, as if she were inviting me to imagine the domestic argument between them, the dinner theater of her feminine deference to his masculine authority—Mark was not, in my experience, any kind of a scold—a brief instant in which she forgot her sorrow and was amused.

Another moment and the mirth faded. She frowned, folding her hands in her lap. Her manner was careful, clearly she wished to rectify the impression created by the passions she had expressed the previous day, and about which she was now apparently so contrite.

They aren't true. And in any case you obviously knew nothing about them.

She spoke with deliberation, nonetheless I was aware that her words did not make much sense, these things that were not true and about which I did not know (how could I have known about them, if they were not true, what would there have been to know about? Or did she only mean that I did not have the false suspicions, had not heard the false rumors?). She looked tired, no doubt she had not slept very well. I looked away.

Let's not talk about that.

Isabella and Mark also had things to hide, I was not the only one. How unforgivable it would have been, if I had not known. I did not see how I could say to her that her declarations had been no more than the confirmation of what I already knew, what I had willed myself not to know for many years, until it was no longer sustainable or believable even to myself. There were arguments to be made—that monogamy is unnatural, it almost certainly is, but then a good many people manage it or something close to it, at the very least they try. Had Christopher also tried? It was possible, or at least it wasn't impossible—but it was no longer the time to make those arguments. That had passed.

Isabella did not, in any event, look as though she felt particularly guilty, her contrition was neither a sincere nor a lasting emotion. The waiter brought our breakfast—a large tray covered in toast and orange juice and poached eggs and bacon for Isabella, who ate with startling appetite. I thought her distress might have overcome her appetite but like so many English people she had an excellent and unflagging constitution.

I sat opposite her as she consumed what would be considered a large meal under any circumstances and a positively enormous one given the present situation, her strong teeth crunching through the toast, bacon and eggs. She wiped delicately—the pretense of delicacy after such a display of appetite was absurd, but it was in character, both the pretense and the delicacy—at her lips and then lowered her napkin to the table.

How quickly do you think they will make an arrest?

I was startled by the question. She had not hitherto brought up the criminal investigation, or even the fact that her son had not simply died but been killed, in fact murdered, and there was a hard brightness to her voice that made her seem even more brittle. Usually people have only one unspeakable fact to contend with in these situations, namely the fact of death, but in this case there was the added unspeakable: the violent nature of this death, this killing, this murder.

I don't know.

What did they say at the police station about the investigation?

I realized then that I had neglected to ask the police chief about the investigation, not even a single question. It was inexplicable, a telling omission, for which I could not account, certainly not to Isabella. *How quickly do you think they will make an arrest?* I thought again of Stefano, who had reason to hate Christopher and who had driven him, *a couple times* by his own account. Isabella would be seeking not only justice but vengeance, it is always the mothers who are the most bloodthirsty, and Isabella would expect me, Christopher's wife, to desire the same.

They weren't able to tell me very much, I said. The investigation is ongoing.

I understand that. But they must have suspects. No doubt.

But nothing they could share with you.

I was there to identify the body.

She drew a sharp breath and leaned back into her chair, I reached a hand out to steady her. Her arm was more fragile than I expected, Isabella wore dramatic and voluminous sleeves, you never saw the limbs themselves, only the beautiful sleeves. It took me by surprise, I could have snapped her elbow between my fingers. After a moment, she reached her hand up and gripped mine.

Of course, my dear. That must have been horrid.

Horrid meant nothing as a word, but her voice was faint, I had been right, it would have been too much to ask this woman, who was older than she seemed, to look at Christopher's body. I was now the one to feel contrition, I had invoked Christopher's body in order to avert confrontation, this was despicable. Isabella cleared her throat and withdrew her hand, a cue for me to remove my own hand, which I did.

Mark is useful in these situations, any man would do better than a woman—this is Greece, after all. They're terribly sexist.

She had become solicitous, even maternal. My

evident distress, she presumed at the memory of Christopher's body, had in some way reassured her, as if it were a relief not to dwell on her own turbulent emotions.

We both loved him, she said. That will always be something that we share, no matter what happens.

This was a very personal thing to say, but she was not looking at me as she said it, she was looking over my shoulder, as if watching someone approach. I turned—I thought it might be Mark, or perhaps the waiter—but the terrace was empty, she was staring at nothing. She then turned back to the water, still wearing the same abstracted expression she had worn when proclaiming our shared love for Christopher, as if it were the expression she considered appropriate for talking about love, love and Christopher.

We will need to decide what to do with the body.

I did not want to use the word *body* and yet I did not know what else to say—it would have been morbid to refer to the corpse as Christopher, it was assuredly not Christopher, but instead an object of decaying flesh and bone, an object of no small horror, *it*. And yet there was a coarseness to my statement that I did not like, if there had been euphemisms at my disposal I would have happily used them, all of them, as many as required. Isabella nodded.

It—she accepted this dehumanizing word,

she reverted to it as I had—will be sent back to London, of course. I cannot imagine cremating Christopher here, much less burying him, what would be the purpose? This is not a place that had any particular meaning to him. He just happened to be here when he was killed. I have no intention of ever returning to this place.

We will need to go to the police station. There will be some formalities.

She frowned.

I think we should send Mark. He can deal with that. Like I said, the Greeks are terribly sexist.

At that moment, Mark finally appeared on the terrace. He was a large and rather impressive man, who took care of his appearance, even now he was dressed like a typical Englishman abroad, in light-colored linens and a straw hat, as if he were mainly on holiday and incidentally collecting the body of his son. Only upon closer examination—as he made his way across the terrace and toward our table—did the grief become visible in his face, and I had a vision of Mark, moving through their apartment in Eaton Square, mechanically packing his bag for a visit he could not have imagined, much less foreseen, one day earlier.

The practicalities of the task would have been a comfort to him, I knew Mark well enough to say that. He would have checked the temperature in Gerolimenas on his computer, he wouldn't have known the place offhand, he would have had to look it up on a map. Then, he would have taken out his suitcase and placed it on the bed before picking out his shirts and trousers and jackets, enough for as long as a week, because he did not know, at that point, exactly what awaited him in Greece.

Despite Mark's generally patient nature, I thought the difference in their manner of grieving might easily open up a chasm between the couple, I could imagine his response to Isabella's grief, he might have thought or even said to himself, Anyone would think from her behavior that Christopher was her child alone. And his mind might have returned to an old and lingering doubt: there was no particular likeness between Mark and Christopher, who looked entirely like Isabella, as if he had sprung from her womb without interference from any third party.

The matter raised certain possibilities, Christopher and even Mark had once said as much, and I remembered thinking it was lucky for Isabella that there hadn't been anything like paternity tests in those days. Not that Mark would have subjected himself to the indignity of scientific evidence—and Mark had always loved Christopher, this was obvious at first glance. The situation was evidently passable, although Mark might not have come to this position immediately, there might have been a lengthy period during which he had considered leaving Isabella, however inconceivable such a thing might appear now.

But even as he had reconciled himself to the life he shared with Isabella—who had only a brief spate of fidelity that lasted until Christopher was about five, that is to say, of an age to notice—I thought surely the possibility had continued to haunt him, just as it had haunted Christopher, the only infidelity that mattered being the one that may or may not have produced the son. He would not have looked for signs of a current liaison, a betrayal in the present tense, but for remnants of an affair long buried, whose possible evidence lived and breathed and grew before his eyes. For years he would have waited for the phone call, the appearance at the door of a man whose face would finally confirm Christopher's errant paternity, another man suddenly visible in his son's features, the stamp of a face that, once seen, could never be unseen again. A man who would then—what? What would Mark have feared?

Perhaps simply that he would be crowded out, as Isabella had crowded him out many times before, as she was doing even now. But that was assuming, assuming the speculation was true. And we would not know, Isabella would never tell, unless she were to make a deathbed confession—whereas there had been no deathbed for Christopher, he had never known for certain, death had taken him, taken all of us, by surprise. I imagined Mark, struck by another wave of unbearable grief, standing in the darkened apartment. In the end there was nothing in the world, he might have thought, so thin, so foolish, as infidelity.

But none of this could be confirmed or even seen on Mark's face as he made his way across the terrace to the table, his straw hat on his head—he looked merely tired, out of sorts, in mild bad humor. I rose to greet him and he patted me on the shoulder, his manner friendly but absentminded, before sitting down next to Isabella.

We've eaten already, I'm afraid, she said.

It doesn't matter. I'm not hungry.

Well, do order something. You need to keep your strength up.

He ignored her but perused the menu with a grumpy expression, no, Christopher's death had not caused the fissures in their relationship to heal or even temporarily conceal themselves. Over the years I had seen that they had an alarming capacity to be rude to each other, even when they were with others, it must have reached extreme levels when they were alone. He put down the menu and signaled to the waiter, who promptly appeared, Mark had that effect on most people, although not on Isabella, she sniffed and turned her face back to the sea.

I've ordered a taxi to take us to the police station, Mark said, once the waiter had gone. We'll need to make arrangements.

I don't want to go, darling, Isabella said. Surely there's no need.

He stared at her for a long moment, as if making some internal calculation, then shook his head and said, Fine. He turned to me. Will you come? Or shall I go alone. I'm happy to go alone.

From across the table, I saw that he had buttoned his shirt up incorrectly, so that the fabric puckered in the middle of the shirt's placket, an unusual slip in a man so fastidious about his appearance, it was an indication of how distraught he was, he could hardly have looked in the mirror before leaving his room. I was embarrassed, it was as if the man had thrown his arms about my neck and commenced weeping. Mark nodded to the waiter as he brought him his coffee, laid out a little jug of warm milk and a bowl of sugar.

I'll go with you to the station, I said.

He looked up, startled.

Fine, he said. Good. Thank you.

The pucker gaped even wider as he leaned forward to drink his coffee, holding the cup in both hands. He had large and rather beautiful hands, fine-boned but still masculine, hands that were not in fact unlike Christopher's, I thought. Isabella took no notice of Mark's hands, I supposed she'd had a lifetime to notice them.

What will you do while we are gone? Mark asked her.

She shrugged and then gave a little gasp, there is a great deal to arrange, she seemed to indicate, and no doubt this was true, I had already told her, when it became apparent that she wished to take control of the funeral arrangements, that she should feel free to do so. She had appearances to maintain in London, whereas I had none. And she had patted my hand again and said that she thought it best, I was too overwhelmed to take on such a task and besides, I didn't know the people to contact, it was much easier if she did it.

I'm older than you, she had said, I'm afraid I've had recent experience in organizing such things.

And she had paused, perhaps remembering friends, family, recently deceased, the phone call informing you of the bad news, perhaps it was sometimes secondhand—a hushed *do you remember so and so,* an obituary in the newspaper—in any case, death was all around you at a certain age. Even just an actor you vaguely remembered from the movies, two years younger than you at the time of death according to the newspaper article. However, you would never expect for your own son to die. She had been looking the wrong way, the death she had been watching for had come from behind.

You must get them to release the body, Isabella was saying to Mark. As quickly as possible.

I imagine they'll release the body when they are ready to release the body, he replied. Have they conducted the autopsy? There was a head wound, Mark said.

Stop! Isabella said, and she covered her ears in a gesture that was childish and somehow offensive, it was hardly a time for such theatrics. But she was right to stop her ears, once she was told the particulars of Christopher's death, there was the danger that this would become the overriding thing, not just of his death, but of his life. Everything that came before—her memories of him as a child, his wit and exuberance, his charm, even as a child he had been able to charm her— all that would fade, it would pale against the incontrovertible finality of the wound to his skull, the wordless violence that silenced everything else.

As quickly as possible, she repeated, lowering her hands from her head. And we'll get him back to England. One of the worst things about this whole—she waved her hand through the air, indicating the breakfast table, the terrace, the sea and the sky—situation is the fact that his body is lying in a strange police station in rural Greece. It will be better, I will feel better, once we have him safely home.

Safely home, and then what? But that was not a question they could understand, for Isabella and Mark the course they would follow was clearly demarcated, painful as it was, grief had a familiar path, it was easy to believe in the specificity of one's grief but in the end it was a universal condition, there was nothing unique about sorrow. Isabella and Mark would return home with their son's body and they would mourn him, his unnatural death and his too brief life. But what would I do? How and who—husband, ex-husband, lover, deceiver—would I be grieving?

10.

Stefano stepped out of the car, he was wearing a button-down shirt and had not shaved. His expression, as he greeted us, was polite and somewhat sheepish, he looked, in the bright sunlight, entirely innocuous, suddenly my suspicions of the previous day seemed nothing short of absurd. I noticed, for the first time, that he was a small man, shorter and slighter of build than Christopher. The evident intensity of his emotions had built him into a larger figure than he actually was, in reality, Christopher would have easily overpowered him.

Still, as we stood outside the hotel, and I greeted Stefano, I felt Mark tense beside me. *This is the kind of man who killed my son,* I could see the thought pass through his mind. As Stefano opened the doors for us, Mark's distaste seemed to increase. I introduced the two men. Stefano's face grew reserved, it was as if he looked at Mark and saw not simply a bigoted foreigner—although he would have also seen that, Mark shook Stefano's hand with an expression of both disdain and consternation, impossible to misapprehend—but the father of his rival.

Was there any likeness between the two men, between Mark and Christopher? It was always said that there was not, but the impression the two men made was not dissimilar. The same confidence and ease and entitlement, perhaps all Englishmen would seem that way to Stefano. He shut the door behind us and got into the driver's seat. As he sat down, he glanced at Mark in the rearview mirror, his expression guarded, as if the father might now steal the affections once possessed by the son.

Mark ignored him, gazing out the window as we drove out of the village with a fixed expression of contempt. Is this from the fires, he asked. I nodded. He shook his head and then stared straight ahead. Once we had gone he would never return to Mani, likely he would never return to Greece. The entire place would be a dead zone for him, contaminated by this single incident, as it had been for Isabella. He looked at the scorched earth, no doubt it was all he could do not to declare this place a hell and be done with it.

That impression could not have changed as we arrived at the police station, which was busier than the day before but had not lost its air of lassitude. There were people in the waiting room who looked as if they had been waiting there for hours if not longer, a man with an open wound to his head was sitting quietly in the corner, he must have been there to report a crime, another mugging perhaps, in different circumstances Christopher might have arrived at the station in a similar condition. Mark stared at the man and his wound, the ghost of his child, he flinched and turned away.

Stefano remained outside with the car. He had insisted on waiting—a gesture of concern on his part, which Mark appeared to interpret as an act of menace or calculation. Stefano stood by the car as Mark walked toward the station in silence. As I passed, Stefano looked at me with an expression of mute pleading and something else I could not identify, it left me unsettled. As we entered the station Mark asked why we couldn't simply call for a cab once we were done, it would cost a fortune to keep the driver waiting and in any case he wasn't sure he liked the look of him. I was saved from replying by the appearance of the police chief, a man I had not seen before, he quickened his pace when he saw Mark, Isabella had been right.

He introduced himself—speaking to both of us but addressing Mark—and offered his condolences, which Mark impatiently waved away. With a sweep of the hand and a politely enunciated *Please,* the police chief escorted us to his office. Mark sat down without being asked, the police chief asked if we would care for a coffee, a glass of water. Mark shook his head, brushing invisible dust from his trousers, a small gesture indicating dissatisfaction. At the same time, his hands were trembling, soon his fingers were compulsively tracing and retracing the seam in his trousers.

The police chief sat down behind his desk and clasped his hands together. His eyes were on Mark's trembling fingers.

We will release the body today. I assume you will be bringing the body to London?

Mark nodded.

It will need to be embalmed before it can be taken out of the country. This is required by the airlines. There is a funeral home in Areopoli— He wrote a name and number on a piece of paper and slid it across the table. Kostas should be able to help you.

Kostas—

The concierge at your hotel.

Mark took the paper, stared at it a moment and then folded it in half.

I've already informed the British Embassy. There will be an inquest.

Of course. There generally is, in such cases.

What can you tell me about the investigation?

The police chief leaned back into his chair, he looked at me briefly before looking back at Mark.

We have faced some terrible budget cuts in recent years. Matters with the central government are nearing a state of emergency, I'm sure you have read about it in the newspapers.

I don't see what that has to do with Christopher's death.

The police chief nodded.

It has nothing to do with your son's death. But it has a great deal to do with the investigation into your son's death, that is to say, our chances of apprehending the person—we assume man, but of course it could also be a woman, and indeed it could be persons, more than one—who killed your son.

He sighed and leaned forward.

People go missing, people are even killed, and many times the culprit is never found. This office—He gestured at the metal cabinets against the wall. It is full of unsolved cases. Investigations that are closed without a satisfactory solution. I'm afraid we do not have the best record.

This cannot be the case with Christopher's death.

I wish I had arrived at the crime scene earlier than I did, but unfortunately I was in Athens, I was visiting my family. At this point we don't even have a suspect, usually with a dead husband you look at the wife, but in this case—

He nodded in my direction, then continued.

Of course, not very much time has passed since your son's death, in many ways this conversation is premature. We will do our best. It is in our own interest. You can imagine, a wealthy foreigner found dead in the street, it makes people feel unsafe. There were rumors that there was a woman involved—

Mark half rose in his seat. He grew flushed as I turned to look at him, I realized it was not only the outrage of the police chief having raised Christopher's infidelity before me, the betrayed. In the idea of Christopher's faithlessness there must have been a reminder of Isabella's own lack of fidelity, as if the trait were inherited, and therefore in some way both inevitable and fated—not simply Christopher's infidelity but this situation, and by extension his death.

—but we discovered nothing, the rumors remained unsubstantiated, although we interviewed all the likely candidates, a jealous husband would have solved the case for us. Unfortunately, this did not come to pass, it does not seem as if there was any relationship between the killer and your son.

Was it my imagination, or did Mark's body relax at that moment? As if his child had been restored to him. I turned once more to look at him but he did not move, he did not return my gaze, it was as if I were not there. After a brief pause, the police chief continued.

I am only attempting to give you the full picture of the case. I do not know if you intend to stay here in Mani, but I must advise you that I do not expect this matter to be resolved at once. If there is any kind of breakthrough, we will of course inform you immediately. He paused again. For now, I think you should return to England, with your son.

Briefly, Mark's shoulders slumped—I nearly asked if he was okay—but then he straightened, he asked if I would leave the two of them alone. I rose to my feet and nodded, I said that I would wait in the hall, in the lobby. Without turning to look at me, Mark said he would not be long. I lingered at the door for a moment, hesitating, but neither man looked up.

I watched the two men sitting across from each other. I had not yet said anything to the police about Stefano, if not a jealous husband or even lover, then a jealous friend, a jealous man, perhaps the one who would have *solved the case for us,* I knew he had sufficient cause for envy. But it did not seem possible to mention this before Mark of all people, he would have mostly felt this to be an accusation against his son, perhaps in some ways it was—Christopher was not, after all, without guilt in this scenario.

And jealousy in and of itself was not the same as guilt. It would take only a small gesture on my part—the articulation of a fear, which was perhaps not the fear that the driver had killed my husband, but the fear that Christopher's betrayals went further and deeper yet, that they would continue to reveal themselves, long past his death—to ruin a man's life, such a thing was not to be taken lightly. I stood at the door, I could not even confirm to myself what it was I thought I knew, Christopher had slept with Maria, but then he had likely slept with several women here in Mani, there might have been multiple men in Stefano's position, I had nothing but a vague suspicion.

I returned to the waiting area. For the first time, I was conscious of being widowed, of lacking the protection of a man, it was an entirely atavistic sensation. Here in the lobby of this police station in Greece, I suddenly felt extraneous to the workings of the world, which is to say the world of men, I had grown invisible, standing at the threshold of that door. I sat down in one of the plastic chairs. The man with the head injury had disappeared, it occurred to me now, how strange it was that he had come to the police station without first tending to his wound, he should have gone to a hospital or a doctor, perhaps there wasn't a local hospital or perhaps it was necessary to first lodge the complaint, certainly you would be more effective in doing so if you were bleeding from the head. If only Christopher had been able to do the same.

Still, as I sat there, even as I felt the essential injustice of his death—perhaps all deaths were unjust, but some were more so—I could not imagine a denouement such as the police chief had evoked only to negate again: the revelation of a jealous husband or boyfriend, someone in

Stefano's position, a man in search of revenge. The idea was abhorrent, not simply because it exposed Christopher's own infidelity, but because of its patent absurdity, the image of a man who had been cuckolded, possessed with the impulse to kill, that man would have come with a knife or a gun, he would not have planned to kill with a rock of all things.

No, it was almost certainly as it had appeared from the beginning: a robbery, both a stupid and a simple death. I thought it likely, however, that Mark would persuade the police chief that a culprit must be found, he would incentivize the situation, wasn't that what happened in these cases? I was about to rise to my feet and go back into the room when Mark appeared. His face was grim and he only said, Let's go.

I followed him out of the police station, once we were in the car and before I could stop him, he said, They will continue the investigation, but I am not hopeful. They appear to have no leads, not even one. I don't know how I'm going to tell Isabella, I don't know what she will do.

Stefano was watching us. I had felt he was listening to our conversation, as soon as I met his gaze in the rearview mirror his eyes flicked back to the road, but not before I saw some complex emotion pass across his features, not before Mark saw him too. He leaned forward without warning and shouted, Why are you

198

listening, why are you eavesdropping? What does my son have to do with you?

I gripped Mark's arm and he leaned back into his seat and then he began sobbing, he said again, I don't know what Isabella will do, I don't know what she will do. I embraced him as well as I could, he was a large man and the car was bumping along the road. He held my hand as he continued sobbing, my arms around him. I looked up and my gaze met Stefano's, we watched each other for several long seconds and then he dropped his gaze back to the road in front of him.

How is Maria? I asked him.

Although he did not look at me, I saw from his reflection in the rearview mirror that he was startled. She is fine, he said after a moment, she is okay. He still looked uneasy, he had been caught off guard, I continued watching him in the mirror but he did not meet my gaze, he was looking at the road ahead, perhaps it did need his attention, the surface was in terrible condition.

Deep down, Stefano must have known that Christopher was only the external manifestation—like ectoplasm from a medium's mouth—of the deeper and more intractable deadlock between him and Maria, the problem of his unreciprocated love. I continued watching Stefano, as we drove out of the village and toward the hotel, Mark's body heavy in my arms. What was the meaning of the relief I had seen in his face, when he had been listening to Mark, was it the fact that there were no suspects, very little evidence, a net with plenty of holes, through which he might yet escape? Could it have been, as he drove us back to the hotel, that he sat in the front seat with his feeling of relief—the police didn't have a clue, they didn't even know that Maria had seen Christopher just before his death—and his belief that he was still a free man?

A free man. Who soon would carry on with his slow courtship, who once again had all the time in the world. Maria would be in need of comfort, and Stefano would be in an ideal position to provide it. If he was smart he would not denigrate Christopher too much (*that scum, he got what was coming to him*) but would be kind, sensitive, entirely forgiving (*what a terrible and unfathomable thing, a man in the prime of his life, no, I couldn't have wished such a death on anyone*).

And if he was patient, if he was not too pushy (as was his wont, this was his fatal flaw, but perhaps he had learned a thing or two), she would eventually turn to him. Because however insubstantial the affair with Christopher—and for all I knew it had been nothing more than a night, two nights—his death would have left a hole in her life. Where previously there had been the fantasy of love, of escape, the excitement of an unknown man, there was now nothing, a woman could coddle a fantasy for only so long, particularly a dead one.

And then there would be space for Stefano. Perhaps it would not even take that long—once you had made up your mind, if Maria were to make up her mind, then things progressed very quickly, perhaps that was even why she had been so reluctant, knowing that once she gave in to Stefano, the remainder of her life would be delineated in an instant, the entire future known. She was young, it was only natural that she would fight against such certainty.

Whether he was guilty or innocent, I knew that he sat in front of us in an agony of anticipation, which he was struggling to conceal, he had hopes for the future, or rather a single hope, which might yet prove foolish. But it was closer than ever before, just within his grasp, a fact of which he could not help but be aware, and so he sat in the car, trying to maintain an appropriately funereal air—after all, there was a grown man crying in the backseat—while a symphony of excitement welled inside him. He reached back with a tissue, which I accepted in silence and passed to Mark, he blew his nose into the paper and said, to me, to Stefano, Thank you.

I left Mark to tell Isabella. He went up the stairs very slowly—if he went slowly enough then perhaps he would never arrive at the top, never have to confront his wife—it was clear he dreaded telling Isabella about the investigation, or rather the lack of it, the whole thing already dead in the water, that he was fearful of her response, there would be a scene, hysterics, she would not take the news lying down. She would upbraid Mark, the nearest and most obvious target, insisting that he go further into the matter (Lady Macbeth, chastising her lord), and yet Mark had said, There's nothing to be done, and I believed him.

But had everything been done, truly everything? Inside my room, I hesitated and then picked up the telephone and dialed the police station. I was put through to the police chief at once—I did not identify myself on the telephone, there was no need, they knew who I was, there were not so many Americans here—and he answered with a wary, Yes? I told him that I had a piece of information, that might or might not be relevant, but given that they were looking for a woman, the signs of an affair, or had been—

Yes?

He was growing impatient. I opened my mouth but did not speak. Yes? he said again. Abruptly, I told him that Christopher had been seen in Cape Tenaro with another woman. Perhaps my voice caught, or I sounded ashamed. He asked me why I did not tell him earlier, and I said that I hadn't wanted to tell him in front of Christopher's father, He has illusions about his son that should be preserved, illusions that I no longer have, and the police chief was silent for a moment and then said, I see.

But do not worry, he continued, we know about this woman, it was a casual friendship, he left her behind in Cape Tenaro, where she remained. There is no husband, no brother or father, and the woman herself has a perfect alibi, another man.

I was silent. The police were more competent than they pretended, which made the case more and not less hopeless—there were fewer unexplored avenues or possible solutions—but what had unnerved me was the sudden disclosure of information about the woman, another lover of Christopher's, until that moment entirely abstract but now on the precipice of becoming concrete. I only had to ask and I would know more about her, perhaps even her name, already I knew that she was unmarried, without a father or brother, that she lived in Cape Tenaro and was promiscuous, at least by certain standards.

A crime of passion is something you read about in books. And although your husband—the police chief paused—seems to have involved himself with the local population, I do not think this is anything other than what it appears.

There were others, I said.

There was a long pause.

Yes, he said at last. But I can only repeat: I do not think this is anything other than what it appears.

I hung up shortly after. A red light pulsed as soon as I put the receiver down. I picked up the receiver again, there was a message from Yvan, I would need to call him back. I dialed his number, he answered at once.

What is happening? I've left three messages for you.

I'm sorry.

Is everything okay?

Yes. Isabella and Mark are here, there has been a lot to do.

Of course.

I think we'll be coming back soon.

What about the investigation?

They don't expect to find the killer.

How so?

They have no leads. No suspects, no real evidence—the police chief more or less told us that the investigation was stalled, he told us that we should not get our hopes up.

Yvan did not say anything and I continued, In some ways it would be easier, if there was no known killer, if Christopher had been a victim of circumstance only. If we could say instead, it's the fault of the situation.

I paused, but Yvan was silent.

Are you still there? I asked uneasily.

Yes, he said. I'm still here.

Okay.

Go on.

There's nothing more to say.

What will you do?

That's not up to me, I don't think.

You're his widow, Yvan said. You're his wife.

I was silent.

You haven't told them, have you?

How could I?

Will you? Is it even important anymore?

I don't know.

Legally you are his wife.

Legally, according to one set of laws, but according to another—

What other?

I mean our own internal laws, we try to do what is right.

And according to those laws—

I let Isabella and Mark decide. Although I do so without letting them suspect that I am anything other than Christopher's wife, his widow.

Because they would be hurt.

Because I—because we—can allow them that much, surely. They have certain illusions that I think they should be permitted to preserve—I used that phrase again—so many having been stripped from them, for example the illusion that as a parent, you do not have to bury your child.

Is this about Christopher?

I don't understand.

I mean is this for Christopher's sake, not Isabella and Mark's, is all this for Christopher? He paused. Christopher is dead, the bonds of the promise you made to him no longer hold.

I was silent. Outside, a group of men sat in one of the tavernas, facing toward the sea. It must have been later than I thought, the sun was beginning to dip down toward the water and the men were drinking, perhaps they had been drinking for a while. They were far away, too far to make out their features—anyway it was unlikely that I would recognize them, I had seen no more than a handful of people in the village, I was still a stranger here. But I could hear the sound of the laughter, they were obviously having a good time.

Are you there?

Yes, I said.

He was right, of course. In *Colonel Chabert*, Balzac's story of a husband returned from the dead—a work I had once translated, although not with particular success, I had not been able to find the correct register for capturing the peculiar density of Balzac's prose, I generally translate contemporary fiction, which is an entirely different affair—the colonel of the title is presumed dead in the Napoleonic Wars. His wife promptly remarries, she believes legitimately, becoming the Countess Ferraud. Then the colonel returns, effectively from the dead, derailing her life completely, and that is where the narrative begins.

Although the story favors the colonel—the countess is the villain of the story, insofar as there is one, she is portrayed as callow, manipulative and superficial—as I worked on the translation, I found myself increasingly sympathetic to the countess, to the extent that I began to wonder if this feeling showed in the translation, if I had weighted the words without realizing it. Of course, this sympathy might not have been so errant, it might have been Balzac's intention, the very effect he wished to cause in the reader: after all, what a terrible fate, to be faithless, to commit bigamy without being aware of it, it was all in the text itself.

Perhaps because of this concern—one that is in the end a question of fidelity, translators are always worried about being *faithful to the original,* an impossible task because there are multiple and often contradictory ways of being faithful, there is literal fidelity and there is *in the spirit of,* a phrase without concrete meaning— I thought about Chabert now. In this case it was not the unexpected arrival of the husband but his unexpected departure that led to a crisis of faith, death rather than life causing the return of the undesired relationship, the reopening of what was once thought closed.

Wasn't that what Yvan feared? That we would sink beneath the weight of this rubble, the line between death and life was not impermeable, people and matters persisted. The return of Chabert is essentially the return of a ghost—it is only Chabert who does not realize that he is a ghost, that he does not belong with the living, and that is his tragedy—a ghost, or rather *homo sacer*: a man without standing in the eyes of the law. Chabert is legally dead; the central character in the book, after Chabert and his treacherous wife or widow, is Derville, a lawyer (the Count Ferraud—Yvan in this situation—is hardly present in the text).

But although we operate under the illusion that there was a single law that regulated human behavior—a universal ethical standard, a unified legal system—in fact there were multiple laws, this was what I had tried to say to Yvan. Wasn't it also the case in *Billy Budd*? Captain Vere is caught between two laws, martial law and the law of God. There is no way of choosing correctly, he is haunted by the death of Billy Budd, *Billy Budd,* the last words of the dying Captain (in the novel, that is; the opera—the libretto written by E. M. Forster—grants Vere life, Forster and Britten having chosen to avoid the operatic cliché of yet another singer keeling over dead in the final act).

It is only when Chabert recognizes that his legal

standing is distinct from his living reality—that he will never be anything but a ghost to the Countess, haunting the living when he should not—it is only when he recognizes the multiplicity of the laws governing our behavior that he allows himself to be relegated to a hospice or insane asylum, and finally accepts his status as *homo sacer*. Chabert relinquishes the very rights he has enlisted Derville to obtain, that is to say, the legal recognition of his status as colonel and husband, he slips down into the cracks, beyond both the reach and the acknowledgment of the law; he ceases to exist.

But Christopher could hardly be called upon to die a second time. And the law remained only too keen to declare the bond between Christopher and myself. We were married, there could be no doubt on that account—and yet we were not, just as the Colonel and the Countess were not, regardless of whatever the lawyer Derville might uncover or prove. And so despite the clear differences, life rarely finds its exact likeness in a novel, that is hardly fiction's purpose, there was a similarity to the situations, a resonance that was the product of the mutual chasm between the letter of the law and the private reality. The question was which to service, which to protect.

Never mind, Yvan said. This is not the time to be talking of such things.

One of the men had risen from his seat outside the taverna and stood by the edge of the embankment, he had his arms extended and he held aloft a glass of some kind. The other men were cheering him on, perhaps he was making a toast or telling a story, they were men in the company of men, it happened less and less, special provision was made for it—the Sunday soccer match in the park, the monthly poker game—but it was not the same thing, it was then a little too orchestrated and self-conscious. I would not see Christopher among that group down on the embankment but perhaps he had been there as little as a week ago, perhaps he had.

The figure that beckons from a previous life—particularly when that life is genuinely good and gone, when it is not a question of real options, a marriage to be repaired, a life to be restored, either right or left, yes or no—can be uncannily persuasive. There is a reason why the living are haunted by the dead, the living cannot haunt the living in the same way. When it is a question of joining the living, you are reminded of all the reasons why you would rather not (or in most cases, as was the case with Christopher and me, you hardly need the reminder). But with the dead, who are sealed off in a separate realm, it is different.

No, I said, we should talk. We should talk before it is too late. And Yvan was silent for a moment and then he said, Okay. Let's talk.

11.

Whatever I said to Yvan, I knew that I would not tell Isabella and Mark about the separation. Not because I wished to protect Isabella, as I had told Yvan, nor out of any loyalty to Christopher, as Yvan suspected, and not because I had made a promise, to him or to myself or to anyone else. I wouldn't for more selfish reasons: because I wanted to pretend that it was as I had led everyone to believe, that there was no separation, no disintegration of our marriage, no pending divorce. It was the desire to continue to exist in the space—suddenly and inexplicably alive—of our marriage.

How much of this reasoning did I understand then, in the days following Christopher's death? I would say that at the time, my own motivations were opaque to me. I acted on poorly defined sensations—what are called *instincts* and *impulses*—at first the only indication of this vast alteration in my feelings toward Christopher, toward our marriage, was the fact that the world of Gerolimenas, in which I was a charlatan, and which was therefore paltry and insubstantial, had nonetheless become more concrete than any other place, as if the world had reduced itself to this single village on this Greek peninsula.

Even more so as the prospect of our departure neared. I saw neither Mark nor Isabella until the next morning, when they appeared at breakfast, looking entirely like themselves, only perhaps slightly more subdued versions. Isabella looked up when I reached the table and then said, without warning, Will you be ready to leave tomorrow? I had not even sat down. There's nothing more to be done here, and I would like to take Christopher home.

She was wearing large sunglasses, which she did not remove (she might have been concealing red and swollen eyes), and she called the body by its name, she called the body Christopher. Previously the body had been *it,* nameless, a small thing that was nonetheless revealing. She had decided to leave and so she had decided to begin grieving, to begin naming things, not as they were—a decaying corpse—but as you wanted them to be—your child, still human, still named and intact.

Isabella said nothing about the investigation—how Mark had persuaded her that there was nothing to be done I still do not know, everything in Isabella's nature would have fought against it. She turned her head restlessly. The decision to let the investigation rest—I assumed for the time being, I assumed the fight would resume once she had returned to England, once she was back on solid ground—had freed her in

212

some way, and I saw that she was ready to leave, to literally move on.

I would like, she continued quietly, still without looking at me although I now sat beside her, to visit the place where he died before we go. She did not say the place where he was killed or the place where he was murdered, she said *the place where he died*. Already the specificity of his death was being sanded down, a gloss was being put on it, not killed and not murdered but died. I don't expect it will help, she continued, but I would like to do that. And then I never want to come back to this place again.

Mark nodded, it was obviously something they had discussed, he even reached across the table and took her hand. The desire to stand in the place where her son had been killed, a place like any other place, death making its claim along a meaningless stretch of road. She would convert that meaningless landscape into something else, it was an act of memorial, she wanted things to become what they were not. The emptiness of death is too hard to sustain, in the end we barely manage to do it for a day, an hour, after the death event itself.

There was something self-serving not only in Isabella's grief, but in all grief, which in the end concerns itself not with the dead, but with those who are left behind. An act of consignment occurs: the dead became fixed, their internal lives were no longer the fathomless and unsolvable mystery they might once have been, on some level their secrets no longer of interest.

It was easier to mourn a known quantity than an unknown one. For the sake of convenience we believed in the totality of our knowledge, we even protected that illusion. At a certain point, if we were to encounter a diary with the record of the dead one's innermost thoughts we would refrain, most of us would not open the book but would return it to its resting place undisturbed, even the sight of it would be horrifying. In this way, I thought, we make ghosts of the dead.

I don't know the place, I said at last.

Mark has arranged a car, Isabella said. She turned to him and pressed his hand, matters between them had evidently improved. We can go in the afternoon, after lunch. Our last lunch in this dreadful restaurant, I must say that I won't miss it. And although I had myself expressed a similar thought, I instantly resented her for it, after all her son had chosen the hotel, it was one of the last things he did. She looked at Mark again and then leaned forward. Now she pressed her hand onto mine and said, Of course, you will be taken care of. Everything goes to you.

I don't think I understood—or one part of me understood, everybody understands the phrase *taken care of,* as well as *everything goes to you,* everything is everything. But another part remained confused, she had changed tack so suddenly, or perhaps my mind was simply being stubborn, refusing comprehension. What did she mean by everything? There was the apartment, of which Christopher had said, when we began talking of a separation and almost in passing, You should have the flat, if it comes to that.

But I had not taken it up with him, although I had already known it would come to that—I did not even know what he meant by *have,* whether he meant that I should stay there while he found another place to live, which was in fact what happened, only I too moved out not long after, leaving the place empty. Or whether he meant that I should take ownership of the apartment— which was what Isabella was talking about, that was what she meant by *taken care of* and *everything goes to you,* she was not talking about personal effects, mementos or memories, she was talking about money.

I withdrew my hand from Isabella's. When we married, Christopher had insisted that we both make wills, a morbid and I thought unusual step to take, although I knew it was common, many of our friends had made similar arrangements after their weddings. Weddings always made your mind go to eventualities and these documents acted as safeguards against those eventualities, unless of course they actually made them come true, the prenuptial agreement that led almost seamlessly to the divorce, the will that led—as it had in this case—to the death, shockingly early and unforeseen.

Had Isabella and Mark already consulted Christopher's will? Was this what he had wanted, *everything goes to you,* or had Christopher— the day he moved out, or earlier even—made an appointment with his lawyer, Circumstances have changed, I would like to amend my will, no longer the same terms or beneficiary. Or perhaps the thought had occurred to him but he had not acted upon it, the matter was hardly urgent— after all, who would he leave the money to? We had no children, he had no siblings, his parents were themselves wealthy.

But if he had changed the will, perhaps the lawyer—Christopher had used the family lawyer, we both had, a reassuring man—had already told Mark and Isabella, Mark would have called him the moment he'd heard news of Christopher's death, he would have called him a second time for advice about the investigation, at which point that lawyer might have said, Christopher called me a month ago, two months ago, he wanted to change his will. The marriage had dissolved, or was on the brink of dissolution. Supposing Isabella and Mark had known the entire time, how would I explain myself to them?

Christopher called me before his trip, Isabella

continued. I didn't tell you this, it didn't seem relevant. Now, of course, I wonder. He left a message, saying that he had something important to tell me.

Her voice was questioning, probing. I was unable to look at her. Christopher must have decided to tell Isabella that we were separated. I leaned back into my seat—it was more upsetting than I would have thought likely or even possible, so it had been truly over for him, with no hope of reconciliation or repair. I must have been flushed or breathing strangely, I felt myself to be on the verge of tears. Mark suddenly leaned forward and asked if I needed some water, I waved my hand to say no. I saw him exchange a glance with Isabella.

She cleared her throat.

Of course, we wondered if you were pregnant, Isabella said. He said that he had something important to tell me. And the fact that you weren't traveling—

I looked at her in bewilderment. She could not keep herself from looking at me with hope, it was another question that was concealed as a statement, *he died loved, we wondered if you were*. I did not immediately reply—I was too surprised, although I shouldn't have been, what else does a mother hope for, when her son gets married, but the issue of progeny? The horror of other people's expectations. And yet I could understand that unruly hope, which would have been made stronger by the premature death of Christopher, her only son.

Her eyes were still resting on my face, it was pure fantasy or delusion, an idea that had passed through her mind—*something important to tell you,* like *taken care of,* is a phrase that seems to have a single meaning, until it doesn't—and then taken root. In her gaze there were shades of both avarice and distrust, I possessed something that she wanted, some kernel of information (was I pregnant or was I not?) or even the embryonic kernel itself, the fantasized grandchild. I was a hope, that something might yet redeem the unfortunate hell of her only son, senselessly murdered, I was the possibility of a continuation that would not undo the death of her child, but might nonetheless in some way mitigate it.

It would be so much better that way. A grandchild, Christopher's child. The child in which the features of the son would be visible, a resurrection of sorts. Also—the thought built into the fantasy from the start, integral to its allure, Isabella would have admitted it to herself, if to no one else—then the money, not just Christopher's money but theirs, all their money, would pass to a descendant, someone they could rightly call an heir. There were no other descendants and I was nothing but a dead end, undoubtedly I would marry again (undoubtedly I would).

I did not blame Isabella for making so callous a calculation—I did not blame her, but I believed her to be capable of it—it seemed natural, perhaps I would have felt the same. And I wished that I could say yes. For a brief moment, it was as incomprehensible to me as it was to Isabella: Christopher was gone and there was nothing, no material remnant—which is what children are, in one sense—nothing but a web of emotions, which would fade with time.

I was not pregnant. The money would not pass from blood to blood. Isabella and Mark would disperse their money amongst various charities.

I'm not pregnant, I said.

She nodded, it was as she had expected, it had only been a hope after all. She lowered her head. As I watched, suspicion crept into her eyes—quickly, as if the emotion had already been lurking, as if it were to hand. I could have told her then—the idea had already half come to her, it was a mere suspicion, but the germ of it had sprung, if I wasn't pregnant, what then had Christopher wanted to tell her?—she would have been upset but perhaps not entirely surprised. It would have been another terrible adjustment, but after the adjustment of death, the idea that her son was no longer alive and in the world, would this secondary adjustment have meant so much, would it have meant anything at all?

I hesitated—the words were simple enough to say, *Christopher and I had separated, that is why I did not come to Greece*—and yet the words were impossible to say, they were repulsive to me, a truth I could no longer bear to articulate. I would have sooner invented some perpetual fiction, an alternate reality, in fact we had been talking about having a child, Christopher had been hard at work on his book, he had been very close to finishing, as soon as he was finished writing we would start trying in earnest.

Abruptly, she turned away.

It's terrible to think that Christopher left nothing behind.

There is his work, I said. He was so close to finishing the book. He came to Greece on his own because he needed to concentrate on his writing, he got so much more work done when he was alone.

There is his work, she repeated.

Perhaps we could set up a fund in Christopher's name.

Isabella sniffed.

A fund for what? I find that I'm tired of foundations and scholarships. They never really commemorate the person. We can talk about this later, Isabella continued after a brief pause. I only wanted you to know that your situation is in no way precarious, I can't imagine that you earn a great deal of money from your work, but it's the last thing you should be worrying about, in the current circumstances.

And I saw that contrary to what I had previously imagined, the tie between us would not simply dissolve, that it would persist for some time. There were material things that kept us together, as the bereaved, even without a child. There would be lunches with Isabella and Mark, telephone calls, this money that I was being offered, that was not rightly mine. It formed one link in a chain that would not break, throughout I would be playing the role of the grieving widow. A part I was already playing—the legitimated version of what I was, my grief, my emotions, labeled and adequately contained.

But in reality, my grief was not housed, and it would remain without address. I would be constantly aware of the gap between things as they were and things as they should have been, afraid that it would show its face in my own, in my way of speaking about Christopher, I would be constantly reminded of how inferior my record of love was to a stronger and more ideal love, one that would have sustained the marriage, even in the face of Christopher's infidelities, a love that could have saved him. I could have been more self-sacrificing, I could have shown the kind of love that Isabella would have expected, that Isabella did expect, to see in the wife of her child.

How many times are we offered the opportunity to rewrite the past and therefore the future, to reconfigure our present personas—a widow rather than a divorcée, faithful rather than faithless? The past is subject to all kinds of revision, it is hardly a stable field, and every alteration in the past dictates an alteration in the future. Even a change in our conception of the past can result in a different future, different to the one we planned.

We stood up not long after. The car will be here in half an hour, Isabella said. And then tomorrow we will drive to Athens and fly back to London, I've already booked the tickets. Mark has booked the driver you used yesterday—Stefano, I think his name is. I stopped, it was impossible for Stefano of all people to drive us to the site of Christopher's death, I placed one hand on her arm.

What is it?

Would you ask Mark to book a different driver?

But why? I thought you had used him before.

I would prefer another driver. He made me—I hesitated, I did not know exactly what to say—uncomfortable.

It was the right thing, a word that said nothing but insinuated much, immediately Isabella was sympathetic, she linked her arm through mine. Yes, of course, she said. It is difficult being a woman on one's own, men can be such a nuisance. Mark will request another driver. I realized, as soon as she said it, that Stefano would interpret the cancellation as a confirmation of his suspicions, Mark was as he appeared, another xenophobe in his country. Nor could I expect my fabrication—although in some ways it was simply the truth, Stefano did now make me uncomfortable—to dissuade Mark's own tendencies to prejudice.

Still, it meant that we would not be driven by Stefano, and that was the important thing, I did not wish to see the driver again. We made our way from the terrace restaurant. As we entered the lobby a peculiar expression crossed Isabella's face, and I stared at her a moment, perplexed. Her eyes were fixed and she had pursed her lips, she looked perturbed and she was pale, almost as if she had seen a ghost.

I turned to see what she was looking at. The lobby was empty, there was only Maria, who was standing behind the desk and looking straight at us, I had not seen her since Christopher's body had been found. I realized that she was not looking at me but at Isabella, with an intensity that must have been startling to Isabella, who of course did not know the first thing about Maria or her relationship with Christopher, who did not know that Maria would look at her and see not a hotel guest, another visitor to these parts, but rather the mother of the man she had loved.

And just as Stefano must have looked at Mark and seen a phantom of Christopher himself,

Maria must have looked at Isabella and seen the feminized and therefore perverted version of her foreign lover, it must have been disquieting to see Christopher in the soft and feminine curves of Isabella's face, the same eyes with the same insistent gaze. They continued to gaze at each other, I watched Isabella's expression change from perplexity to one of vague disdain and disgust, perhaps she thought Maria overly insistent.

Except that it did not appear to be the case, as Isabella continued to look at Maria with an expression of distrust that was too pronounced for a stranger, I began to suspect that she had somehow managed to apprehend (a mother's intuition) the nature of the relationship between Maria and Christopher, the reason for the fixedness with which the girl was now regarding her. It was as if Maria could not look away, as if the sight of Isabella were too fascinating.

Isabella flushed and turned away. She made an audible sound of disapproval, Strange manners that woman has, and I was reassured, it was entirely in my imagination, how could Isabella have guessed at the link between Christopher and Maria, the fact that he had more recently been intimate with the severe young woman standing behind the hotel lobby reception desk than he had been with me, his wife, by a measure of months?

She continued, That's exactly the kind of woman Christopher would have liked. I was startled, despite myself I was impressed, she knew her son well, far better than I had known him, how many times had I seen Maria before I had really seen her? Isabella looked at me with a quizzical expression, as if we were merely discussing the peculiarities of a mutual friend, I shrugged and said that I did not know, I could not say, obviously we had nothing in common, this woman and I. She gave Maria another troubled look and then turned away, as if the matter were closed.

It had been closed, until Isabella had incautiously pried the door open again, however briefly. She clenched her jaw as she proceeded in the direction of the stairs as if to say, Enough, no more, and I saw that her mourning was an act of will, just like everything else with Isabella. She said that Mark would tell the concierge to request a different driver, she asked if I would be ready to go in an hour, and I said that was fine, that I would meet her and Mark in the lobby.

12.

Another driver was sent to escort us on our journey. Mark gave no indication of surprise at having been asked to make the alteration, it was true that the previous encounter had not been felicitous, *uncomfortable* was in fact exactly the word for it. Mark was not the kind of man who liked making a scene and he had done precisely that in the back of Stefano's car.

No doubt he had no intention of doing it again. He sat in the front seat with an abstracted and somewhat dignified mien, without looking at the driver, who had not introduced himself to us. Isabella and I sat in the back. There had been no question of either of us sitting in the front beside the driver, it was Mark's natural instinct for chivalry asserting itself, as though Isabella and I needed to be shielded from the driver, the discomfort of sitting beside a stranger.

As we pulled down the hotel drive, Mark asked the driver if he knew where he was going and the man said yes, Kostas had explained everything to him, he knew the place. As if we were going to a local restaurant or tourist attraction. Isabella looked out the window with a tense and bewildered expression, she still could not understand what had brought her son here, it would never be anything but confounding, no matter how long she stayed in Greece, whether or not she saw the place of his death. In that sense she was right to leave, there was nothing for her to learn or understand here. I heard Mark say to the driver, We want to see the place where our son died.

I still don't know why he said this, he was not the kind of man who was prone to taking strangers into his confidence, he did not have the impulse to ingratiate, nor was he a man for small talk. But although the driver did not respond, apart from a small nod of acknowledgment—it was hard even to know how much English he had, the man had barely spoken a word, he might not have understood what Mark had said, this fantastical statement—Mark continued unprompted, It's something we need to do before we can leave, and the driver nodded again, as if to say that he understood, that he agreed.

Evidently the driver was a good listener, proficient in silences, perhaps it was necessary in this trade, although in my experience it was always taxi drivers who had been the ones to strike up conversation, the ones who had things to get off their chest, hadn't Stefano been like that, at least with me? After a brief silence between the two men, the driver said to Mark, his English almost flawless, These things are important. An empty phrase and yet Mark nodded, his eyes brightening, as if the driver had said something profound, deeply sympathetic.

Perhaps Mark wanted to share his grief with someone other than Isabella, other than me—a stranger, who is without his or her own grief, around which you are not obliged to step, can be of greater comfort than those who are in loss's trench beside you—or perhaps he was enjoying the contact with another man, he was a man who liked to be among other men and he was mourning the loss of his son, it had been the two of them and Isabella and now he was alone in the marriage. Mark continued, You know that my son was killed, and the driver again nodded, yes, a terrible thing, he had two children, he could not imagine anything worse in this world.

Mark turned toward the driver. We could stay, but what would be the point? Our lawyers say that we can continue to pressure the police from London. There will be an inquest in England, the British government will be involved—after all, a British citizen has been killed, it's a matter of some interest. But that will not bring Christopher back. It will not even necessarily find the man who killed him. He paused. The incompetence of the Greek police is a force beyond comprehension.

There is no reason for us to stay. But at the same time it is hard to leave, hard to leave without feeling as though we are abandoning

Christopher—our son, his name was Christopher. We are taking him back with us, he will be buried in England. But even so, I feel as though we are leaving him behind, there is unfinished business here. Isabella was still staring out the window, as if she could not hear a word Mark was saying, perhaps she had grown accustomed to not listening to her husband. I suppose the living will always feel this way, Mark said, everything you do is a betrayal.

This was even more intimate than what he had already said to this man, it had the quality of a confession. He stared at the road ahead, as did the driver, two men staring at a road. After a brief silence—the driver remained silent, as if at last Mark had confounded him—Mark turned to look out the window on his side of the car.

We had driven farther inland than I had been before, through several villages and then onto an empty stretch of road. There was burnt brush on either side of the single-lane road, in amidst it stood clusters of singed cactuses, their arms drooping and partially melted. Through the blackened earth small green shoots were beginning to show, although it wasn't the season for things to be growing, further evidence of madness. It might have been a place like this, between two villages, an evening walk, Christopher was prone to doing such things.

The driver cleared his throat. He must have

been unnerved by Mark's speech, he would have known that it was out of character, not in keeping with the tense and upright demeanor of this Englishman, the stony façade crumbling due to grief. He had been speaking the simple truth when he had said that he could not imagine it— the grief, the loss of the child. We are near, he said, almost reluctantly.

Isabella stiffened, the whole of her body going rigid at once. In front, Mark resumed speaking, as if he had not heard the driver, as if to deny or at least postpone the meaning of his words, he would have liked to keep driving, for hours if possible. No father expects to outlive his son, he said, it goes against nature. But even as he spoke, the driver slowed the car and we came to a halt outside a small village and then Mark did not say anything further. Without the noise of the engine it was suddenly silent. Isabella shifted in her seat.

Is this it?

Her voice was harsh and disapproving, she sounded as if she were being shown a substandard property by an incompetent real estate agent, I'm sorry but this house will not do, it does not meet my needs at all. But there could be no house wide enough for her grief, with an abrupt movement she unbuckled her seat belt and stepped out of the car. Mark sat in the front seat with his hands resting in his lap, he did not look at Isabella, who stood outside with her hand resting on the roof of the car. The driver also opened his door and stepped out, Isabella then moved away from the vehicle.

How do you know this is the place?

The driver looked away. Isabella's tone was imperious, as if grief were a service industry like any other, her experience of grief was failing to meet her standards, she would like to speak to the management. Inside the car, Mark inhaled—a noisy, ragged kind of a breath, the man was gathering himself—and then opened the door and stepped outside. After a moment, I followed, I could not remain in the car, although I would have liked to.

Are you sure this is the place? Isabella insisted.

The driver then nodded, Yes, this is the place, without doubt. I wondered then if he, like Stefano, had chanced to drive by that morning, if he too had seen the roadblocks and the police car, per-haps even the body, or what was visible of the body, *the legs under the tarp, the feet askew. That road is the fastest route between the two villages,* a dozen people must have driven past that morning alone.

I turned to look for Mark and Isabella, they had not gone very far, they were perhaps twenty feet away. They stood side by side, looking out across the stretch of blackened dirt. The horizon was cluttered with telephone wires and abandoned shacks and rusted oil drums, a cluster of squat concrete buildings. Mark and Isabella were still, they were not touching but they were physically close, in some ways more intimate than I could remember seeing them since their arrival in Greece, than I could remember seeing them in recent years.

And yet it did not seem to be a moment of reconciliation, much less one of closure, they looked like an elderly couple who had gotten lost in a foreign place and who could not rely on each other to find their way out, a terrible fight could easily follow, one of them walking off into the distance without looking back, the other remaining by the car, waving a map helplessly in one hand. How has it come to this? What am I doing here? They looked at the black dirt and the charred or wilting vegetation, they might have hoped that it contained clues, but there was nothing, it was a place like any other place, there was nothing they could hope to learn from it.

I watched as they stepped, wobbling—Isabella reached out to steady herself on Mark's arm— off the road, onto the verge. They suddenly looked much older, as if the place and not just Christopher's death had aged them, and for a moment I could have believed that it was haunted, that a malignant spirit had drawn the life out of them, there were many such stories in

Greece, it was part of their tradition. This was, I remembered, what had brought Christopher to Mani—regardless of what Isabella said, *it would have been about a woman, Christopher never could keep his cock in his pants,* the cult of death had drawn him here.

Almost as if he had come here to die. He was not suicidal, Christopher would never have killed himself. But he had come to Mani searching for signs of death, for its symbols and rituals, its obscure leavings, he had looked at this landscape and converted it into a pattern of rites for the dead and dying. How could his own end not have factored into his speculations about death in general, how could its possibility not have occurred to him? It was impossible to contemplate his final days without seeing the pall of death, even his philandering—an irrepressible habit formed over a lifetime—began to look like a vain protest against the end that was impending.

After a certain age, it is a question of mere decades, two or three if you are lucky, hardly any time at all. And feeling this presence of death, how would he have regarded the state of our marriage? Even if he did not regret the separation, he might have been susceptible to the feeling I now had, that we were old to be starting again. Christopher was eight years older than me. What had he seen, when he stood here, in those final moments? Perhaps nothing—perhaps it had only been an ordinary place, the circumstances entirely normal, until the blinding crack on the back of his head.

I looked around me. The feeling had passed, it did not seem like a place where someone we loved had died, it didn't have that intimacy—the way the bed where someone we loved slept, the desk where someone we loved worked, the table where someone we loved ate their supper, had that intimacy, immediately and without effort—rather it was only a desolate stretch of road, desolate but not desolate enough, in the distance you could see the village, crossed with telephone wire, there was garbage in the burnt shrub, at our feet there were crushed beer cans and cigarette stubs.

I stared down at the stubs, all fairly new, their paper only a little yellowed, they were everywhere, they covered the ground. It was extraordinary that people could stand in the middle of this torched landscape and throw a cigarette—perhaps still burning, who knew—to the ground. Maybe they thought the landscape so much destroyed there was nothing to preserve, it was true that there was nothing here, in fact it was inexplicable that someone would have stood here long enough to smoke a cigarette, inexplicable that anyone would be standing on this road at all. Even us, our reason for being here—it became more indefinite by the minute.

I looked up at Christopher's parents. I remembered meeting them for the first time, I had not met Isabella and Mark until Christopher and I were ourselves engaged to be married, by which late point I had already heard a great deal about them from Christopher, almost none of it good. He had spoken about them very little and then he suddenly had a great many things to say about them and their marriage, whether because he was now proposing to get married himself—he was not young when we married, he had managed to postpone it for some time—or simply because that particular box, that repository, Christopher's feelings toward his parents and Isabella in particular, once opened, was difficult to close, it had to spill its contents at least a little bit.

And so I was apprehensive, even more than might be usual—and it is rarely classified as an easy encounter, meeting your future in-laws—although I expected it would not be as bad as Christopher said, he had himself declared, You will probably love them, they are very charming, as if it were a betrayal I had already committed. But I did not love them, and I did not find them especially charming, and that strain had showed in my relationship with them ever since. I remembered sitting across the table from them—one of many interminable dinners, once I was introduced to them it became a regular occurrence, the monthly dinner with Isabella and Mark, without discussion and almost without my noticing, something I never could have foreseen at the outset of our relationship—and thinking how much I hoped that our marriage, Christopher's and mine, would not be like that.

I say hoped. In fact I was blithely confident, it seemed impossible that we could be like Isabella and Mark, I could not conceive of a future that would produce such a dire result. In the end, I had been right, we had not ended up like Mark and Isabella, although not for the reasons I thought then. At the time, I was like any young person looking at an old person—even if I was not that young, and nor was Christopher—and like any person who cannot believe that they will grow old, much less die, I could not believe that our marriage could become like their marriage, much less fall apart completely.

And yet it had, after five years. Five years—a fraction of the length of Isabella and Mark's marriage, which continued, which was continuing now. They stood with one foot of air between them and their marriage accrued further hours, greater length, minute by minute. It might have been a terrible marriage, built on betrayal—although what was really meant by the word *terrible,* there were betrayals that looked unforgivable from the outside and that were nonetheless forgiven, and there were forms of intimacy that looked nothing like the name—but it was nonetheless a marriage.

Whereas mine had ended—twice. It was not surprising that I would now look at Christopher's parents and see their marriage anew. It seemed incredible that I had ever looked at it and seen anything to scorn, the word sounded too strong but it was nevertheless accurate, it was the truth. One of the problems of happiness—and I'd been very happy, when Christopher and I were first engaged—is that it makes you both smug and unimaginative. I now looked at Isabella and Mark's marriage and saw that I understood nothing, about it or about marriage in general, they knew things that Christopher and I had not had, or had not taken, the time to find out.

Abruptly, Isabella turned and came back to the car. I think we are finished, she said. The driver nodded and Isabella climbed into the backseat. Her back was rigid and as she stared at the back of the driver's headrest, I saw that her eyes were glassy with tears. She grimaced, as if she had no intention of letting the grief get the better of her, then straightened her shoulders and said, Mark? Are you coming? I would like to go, I don't want to be here anymore.

Mark nodded to the driver, together they got into the car. The driver hurriedly put the key into the ignition and started the engine, we pulled away with a screech. Isabella's back and head swayed with the motion but the grimace did not go away, nor did the tears. Where should I go, back to the hotel? the driver asked, and Mark nodded, Yes. Back to the hotel. When do you leave Greece? the driver said, and Mark replied, As soon as possible, as soon as we can pack our bags.

13.

That winter, a small cruise ship disappeared in the South Pacific. A meteorologist in New Zealand received a satellite phone call at two in the morning from an unidentified woman, who stated that the ship was in bad weather, gave their coordinates, and asked where they should navigate in order to move away from the storm. The meteorologist, who was covering the night shift, told the woman to call back in thirty minutes, by which time he would have studied the forecast and would be able to advise her.

The woman never called back. Following protocol, the meteorologist raised the alarm. Rescuers initiated a radio search, attempting to contact the boat and the mysterious woman who had placed the initial call, and whose number the meteorologist and rescuers continued to ring in the hours that followed—the phone was not dead, it simply went unanswered. Rescuers then began contacting other boats and ships in the area to ask if they had spotted a vessel in distress, or indeed any vessel at all.

A military plane was next dispatched to survey the area from which the call was believed to have originated. This took place some thirty-six hours after the initial call was made—a communication that was not necessarily a distress call, more a cautionary query, an indication of distress that might yet come—but time at sea is slower than it is elsewhere, on land and in air. The designated area was immense, working from the coordinates given in the initial call, it had a radius of over one thousand nautical miles. For many hours, the plane scanned the pocked and dappled surface of the ocean, but found nothing.

A week passed. Two hundred and thirty-two people were on board the ship, including the captain and crew. The immediate families of the missing persons were flown to Australia during this anxious week of waiting, and remained there—they were put up in an expensive hotel by the cruise company, a small ship corporation that specialized in luxury voyages through the South Pacific—as if geographical proximity might somehow lessen the strain of their anxiety. It was true that many of them were from Europe, in traveling to Australia they traveled twenty hours closer to embracing their loved ones, once they were found and returned to land.

As the search widened—several national governments were now involved, the story was getting a great deal of play in England, the cruise ship company, whose boats boasted spacious cabins and an excellent passenger-to-crew ratio, was popular with retired couples—the families began to tire of their extended stay in Cairns.

Among other amenities, the five-star hotel provided bay and marina views. The sight of the water, however, was hardly soothing. Before long, the luxury served only to remind the families of the fact that they were not at home but in limbo, a state of waiting.

In reality, those weeks were merely an introduction to the months and then years that would follow, during which—even as the search tapered off, and the insurance companies began preparing enormous settlements for the families of the missing passengers and crew—there was no news of the ship, and those on board were neither dead nor alive but simply missing. In the numerous interviews that the families gave (these too petered out, at first the media could not get enough of the story, journalists hounding the families for comment, but then they suddenly lost interest, it was often the case) they spoke about the difficulty of grieving, when they did not know whether they should live in hope or, as one of them put it, *move on*.

One of the reasons why it was so difficult to do this moving on was because of the vastly improbable nature of the ship's disappearance, it was small as far as cruise ships go but large as an object to go missing in this day and age, especially when it had been outfitted with the most current technology and multiple redundant safety features. There was no ready explanation, in fact there had been no actual report of bad weather—which made the phone call from the unidentified female all the more baffling—and no wreckage or debris was ever discovered. The ship had simply vanished without a trace.

There were many theories regarding the disappearance of the ship, ranging from environmental disaster (the ship had literally been swallowed by the sea) to geopolitics (the ship had been hijacked by terrorists). One of the more popular theories that circulated during this time held that the passengers aboard the ship had conspired with the crew to orchestrate their own disappearances. They purchased their tickets, they bid farewell to their families, and then vanished into thin air, central to this theory was the fact that the ship's itinerary included such remote and exotic locales as the island of Vanuatu (known for its natural beauty and its native inhabitants' worship of Prince Philip) and the Solomon Islands.

The notion that all the missing were living together on a tropical island was of course outrageous, and although it was an attractive solution—the missing alive and not dead, and living in relative happiness, on something like an extended holiday in a beautiful place—it was not without its complications, given that it was predicated on the idea that everyone aboard the ship had wanted desperately to escape not only their lives, but all the people in them, that is to say, all the people who had gathered in Cairns in the hopes of being reunited with the disappeared.

But isn't that often the suspicion about the dead? There was, of course, nothing so catastrophic as a missing ship in our case, nor was there any doubt about whether or not Christopher was dead or still living—he was definitively dead, there was no question or hoax about it—but there was still something unresolved about his death. Once you begin to pick at the seams, all deaths are unresolved (against the finality of death itself, there are the waves of uncertainty in its wake) and Christopher's was no exception.

As predicted, the investigation was not successful and the case was closed a little over a year later, quietly and with no notable air of defeat. The police had not expected to find the killer and therefore seemed neither surprised nor disappointed when their investigation did not succeed. I heard the news from Isabella. They have closed the investigation, she said on the telephone. We could push to reopen the case, she continued. But there is no guarantee that we will be any more successful, in fact there is little likelihood of that. There is no evidence, the entire thing was botched from the start. We are ready to close this chapter and move on, she said. But we wanted to ask how you felt.

Her voice was quizzical, perhaps she really was

wondering. To my surprise I found that I did not agree, I was inclined to pursue the investigation, to set in motion whatever legal proceedings would make this possible, as Isabella said, the entire thing had been mismanaged from the start. Perhaps there was a chance we would find the person responsible for Christopher's death, knowledge that would genuinely close this chapter, and genuinely allow us to move on (the language Isabella used was bizarre, not the way she usually spoke, the statement was clearly rehearsed and in bad faith).

Before I could reply, she continued, I also wanted to tell you that Christopher's investments—or rather, the investments Mark made on his behalf—have been wound down, the amount is roughly three million pounds. I was too startled to speak, there had been nothing to indicate that I was due to inherit such a large sum. The lawyer will contact you with all the details. It's not very much, she continued without any audible irony, these days it will barely buy you a house in London. She then rung off abruptly, saying that she was tired, and that we would speak again in a day or two.

That day, I experienced the opposite of closure. By evening the money was rotting in my mind, it was contaminating everything. I did not see how I could accept it and I did not see how I could refuse it. I began to wonder what sum would have been acceptable, would a mere million pounds have troubled my conscience less? Two million pounds? Did it matter, the fact that my own feelings toward Christopher had changed since his death, or the fact that had Christopher been alive and had we proceeded with a divorce—which we would have, undoubtedly—half the money would have been mine anyway, given the fact that I was, according to the language of divorce, the aggrieved party?

People hired lawyers and paid extravagant sums of money to achieve the outcome that had by chance, or rather misfortune, come to pass. I wondered why Christopher had not told me about this money, these investments—when I returned to London I was informed that he had inherited a substantial sum of money two years earlier, at a time when our marriage was still intact, and which Mark had invested on his behalf. I wondered why he had chosen to leave the matter in Mark's hands, perhaps even under Mark's name, I hadn't inquired as to the specifics. It might have been done with a future separation already in mind, in his mind at least—a way to circumvent the division of assets—or it might have been out of sheer lassitude, Christopher didn't need the money.

Just as I had no need of it. And yet it was there, and something would need to be done with it. Three million pounds—I was not mercenary,

I wanted nothing less than to be mercenary in these circumstances, and yet I discovered that it was a sum of money that infected the imagination. A great deal could be purchased with three million pounds, contrary to Isabella's assertions, three million pounds was a great deal of money, it was a new life and not simply a new house, the house that I had begun, despite myself, to imagine.

Perhaps a week after this, I received a Facebook message from Stefano, saying that he and Maria had married, that they were very happy and were thinking about starting a family. I had not been in contact with Stefano, I was in some way amazed that he had thought to find me on Facebook, through an account I rarely used. I clicked and saw that he had posted a set of wedding photos on his profile page, they had been married at the hotel in Gerolimenas, exchanging their vows—it appeared from the photos—on the stone jetty where I had once sat and looked up at Christopher's window.

Over the last year, at various points, I had worried that I had liked Stefano too much, that I had allowed my interest in his plight—which, in retrospect, was no plight at all, a woman does or does not love you—to blind me to his true nature. He had, after all, a clear motive, a motive that was stronger than a handful of worn bills and a watch and wedding ring, sundry charges made to a credit card. He would have had time to plan the murder, he would have had access, the thought must have occurred to him, *Things would be different if he was gone.*

But I at last felt certain that he could not be guilty of killing Christopher, the tone of his Facebook message was happy and relaxed, he posted his wedding photographs freely and without hesitation, photographs that were entirely ordinary. He could never have sent me such a message had he actually killed Christopher. But if not Stefano, then who? Since these coincident events, the phone call from Isabella and the message from Stefano, my thoughts have returned once again to the facts and circumstances of Christopher's death, and to the question of culpability.

Most days, I believe Christopher was killed by a thief, that it was a meaningless and unintended crime and therefore death—although it is hard to know what is worse in these circumstances, a meaningless or a meaningful death. There are days when I think almost incessantly about the thief—who I believe exists, despite the fact that he was never seen or described, much less apprehended, and yet who is now free, entirely embodied, pursuing a life unchanged by the nature of his crime, who perhaps continues to roam the Greek countryside mugging hapless tourists. And it is astonishing to me, the fact that we do not know the first thing about the person who killed Christopher, or at the very least left him for dead.

We do not know what he looks like, we do not know if he has dark or light hair, if it is curly or straight, coarse or fine or neither, if he has a family, if there are children and a wife in a house somewhere in Mani, if he is a small man or a large one, perhaps he is a small man with soft features and delicate skin, why not? Or perhaps he stands six feet tall and his skin is marked with acne scars, this is also possible. The man—in some ways, although none of us will say it, the most important man in Christopher's life, the man who brought him death, just as Isabella gave him life—is a blank.

But we do know, if we dare to imagine, that those final moments will have been intimate, even if the precise nature of that intimacy diverges from what we usually think of when we hear and use the word—the arm thrown around the neck, the hand resting on the shoulder, the lips against the ear and the whispered words. This will have been no tender embrace between loved ones but it will have been intimate nonetheless, the contact between the two men being of the most definite and significant kind, against which all erotic touch fades, including my own, including that of all the others.

Did he see the man, did they speak before he

was attacked—perhaps the man asked a question in order to disarm him, a request for directions, or maybe he asked for change or a light for his cigarette, anything to strike up conversation and make Christopher slow his pace. Or did he spring on him from behind, so that Christopher did not see the face of his assailant, did not look him in the eyes—did not even see the features of his face or the build of his body—the man's only greeting being the blunt force of the rock he wielded, hitting against Christopher's skull.

Not too hard, not with the intention of killing— simply in order to daze and disorient him, enough force to knock him out, nothing about the nature of the blow indicated that murder was the intended outcome of the crime, it was theft and not murder. Most likely the man believed that Christopher was merely unconscious, he would wake up with a terrible headache and a little dehydrated but nothing more, a little less force and Christopher would be here today.

But that is assuming he was killed by a stranger, that is assuming he did not, for example, stumble and hit his head on the rocks below—an unlikely and unfortunate blow but not necessarily an impossible one, stranger things have happened, the autopsy had shown that he had been drinking, that he was inebriated at time of death. In the middle of the night, this possibility is infinitely worse, a death completely without dignity, perhaps what we had feared most during the course of the investigation—an outcome worse than the final, inconclusive one—was the confirmation that there was no killer, that he had died wandering drunk and alone.

An empty and ridiculous death. That is why I sometimes prefer, perversely, the notion that Christopher's death had in some way been brought about by his own actions, unintentional and unknowing as they were. Sometimes it is comforting to think that his death was a result of his being in the world, rather than his death having occurred entirely at random, as if erasing a presence that had already failed to leave its mark, that had not insisted sufficiently upon its life; then it would truly be as though he had vanished into thin air.

No doubt that is why, late at night, other scenarios occur to me—that there was indeed a vengeful and cuckolded husband to some unknown woman who was not Maria, who followed him out of the village—*there were rumors that there was a woman involved, a jealous husband would have solved the case for us*. Wasn't it possible that the investigation failed not because the husband did not exist, but because the village had closed ranks against the police and, by implication, against the idea of justice for the stranger, the outsider, for Christopher? Or perhaps the police themselves had known the parties involved, and had chosen to protect them.

Of course, by morning, these ideas are absurd, and the conjectures that seemed plausible enough by night fall apart. In daylight, I can admit that my imagination was only seeking drama in what was, what has always been, a transparent death. When someone you love dies an unnatural death it is natural to look for a larger narrative, a greater significance, the shock of the event seems to require it. But in the end this is only chasing shadows. The real culpability is not to be found in the dark or with a stranger, but in ourselves. Of all the suspects—scattered among disparate bodies, existing in separate narratives—no one had more motive than I did. I had motive, several motives in fact—a huge sum of money to gain, a philandering and careless husband who had, at least according to appearances, all but abandoned me, another man I wished to marry. The motives had coalesced around me, a mantle manifested by my guilt—the guilt of the living, for which it is impossible to atone.

And yet it appeared to be a matter of indifference to everybody else. We sold the apartment about eighteen months after Christopher's death—I did not want to live there, and Mark and Isabella thought this much the best course—and shortly after, I purchased a house in the same neighborhood, a fifteen-minute walk from where

Christopher and I had lived. Yvan and I are now engaged, and we live in this house, which is too large for us, but which we say we will grow into, perhaps, if we have children, or at least a child. The money Christopher left to me—I still believe inadvertently—sits untouched, something that I think Yvan understands, although I do not know if he thinks this will change with time, in a matter of a year, perhaps two.

I cannot be certain it will change, or even if the relationship with Yvan will last, not out of any reluctance on my part, but on his. Something about the terms of the contract—the agreement that we entered into, unwritten and unspoken but no less binding—have changed, he finds himself living with, and also now engaged to, not a woman newly divorced, but a woman who has lost her husband, and who continues, while trying to conceal it from him, to grieve this loss. Sometimes, lying in bed beside Yvan, I remember being in Greece with Isabella and Mark and worrying that they would spot the rift of my pretense, the artifice of my widow's grief.

But there was less difference than I thought, between the grief that I experienced and what I thought of as the legitimate grief of a legitimate wife—the grief that I attempted, while with Isabella and Mark and then before the world in general, to emulate. The emulation became the thing itself, in the end there was not that much difference between the grief of a wife and the grief of an ex-wife—perhaps *wife* and *husband* and *marriage* itself are only words that conceal much more unstable realities, more turbulent than can be contained in a handful of syllables, or any amount of writing.

They say that there are five stages of grief, that things get worse before they get better, and in the end time does indeed heal all wounds. But what about the wounds you do not know you do not know about, and the course of which you cannot predict? I know that one thing is certain: if Christopher were still alive, I would now be married to Yvan. There would be no regular visits to see Isabella and Mark, no meetings about the setting up of a foundation in Christopher's name (despite her misgivings, Isabella decided that in the end she would like to see a foundation established), no prospective publication of Christopher's second and final book.

There would not be this, or the many e-mails and telephone calls relating to this. There would be no sleepless nights, no reservoir of emotion both unexamined and unknown, which only gathers and grows, a black and nameless pool that petrifies me, on the precipice of which I seem to lie, and of which I speak to no one. Against which my relationship with Yvan—the current relationship, the one that matters, whose details are entirely sunlit, in fact too well lit for my taste, it hurts to look at them, there is nothing I cannot see—is forced to contend.

Sometimes Yvan jokes that it is rotten luck that Christopher was killed and I have to agree, it is terrible luck, for all involved. Yvan said only last week that he did not know how much longer he could wait. And although I could have said, For what?—after all, wasn't I here, in his home, in his bed, and weren't we engaged—I knew exactly what he meant, and I could only say that I was sorry, and that I agreed—although what we were waiting for, what exactly it was, neither of us could say.254254

Acknowledgments

Thank you, Ellen Levine, Laura Perciasepe, Jynne Dilling Martin, Claire McGinnis; Clare Conville, Geoff Mulligan, Anna-Marie Fitzgerald. To those who read and responded to early drafts of this book: Karl Ove Knausgaard, Meghan O'Rourke. Finally, thank you to my first and best reader, Hari Kunzru.

This book was written with the support of the Lannan Foundation and OMI International Arts Center. I am also grateful to Ian Seiter, Stephanie Skaff, and the Hertog Fellowship Program at Hunter College.

Center Point Large Print
600 Brooks Road / PO Box 1
Thorndike, ME 04986-0001 USA

(207) 568-3717

US & Canada:
1 800 929-9108
www.centerpointlargeprint.com